NO MORE FEEDBACK

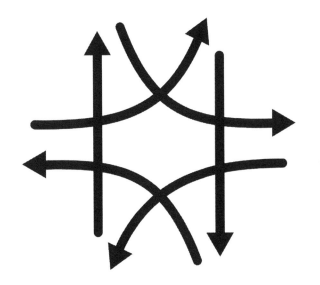

[CULTIVATE
CONSCIOUSNESS
AT WORK]

CAROL SANFORD

InterOctave
535 Walnut. St. No. 201
Edmonds, Washington 98020
www.interoctave.com

ISBN (print): 978-0-9893013-1-2
ISBN (ebook): 978-0-9893013-2-9

Ordering Information:

Special discounts are available on quantity purchases by corporations, associations, and others. For details, contact InterOctave at the address above.

TO THE MILLENNIALS—

We count on each new generation to help us steer toward a better world.
Thank you for stepping up to the plate so ferociously.

ACKNOWLEDGMENTS

This is the first book I have written without my great publisher, Nicholas Brealey. Thank goodness, I always have Kit Brewer, my dedicated and diligent personal editor, who has gone above and beyond on this work. Scott Yeager provided invaluable guidance early on about how to structure the book. A handful of my Change Agent Community members also cared enough to dig in and tell me what worked for them and what did not. Thanks in particular to Jennifer Atlee, Beatrice Ungard, and Mary Emeny. Additional thanks to Gabriel Fehrenbach and Lisa Gill from LinkedIn connections who offered straightforward and useful advice.

I also want to acknowledge the members of my Change Agent Development Community and Regenerative Business Development Community, all of whom are dedicated to their own growth in service to evolving human systems and our effects on Earth through a *regenerative paradigm*. They challenge and inspire me every day.

CONTENTS

FOREWORD

I think the intentions of feedback proponents are pure—compared with the top-down, hardline mandates of the past, having a space for dialogue about performance is a huge step up. Performance reviews, particularly ones using "360-degree feedback" from people at different levels of a company, were meant to be collaborative. But they also came out of the machine reductionist paradigm, in which the world is seen as one giant assembly line, and all you have to do is input x to produce y. Of course, the world is not so simple, and humans are not machines.

In my over twenty-five years of experience in business, I've seen how detrimental constant feedback can be, how it chips away at our powers of discernment and the self-confidence we need to investigate and express whatever it is that makes us unique. I've also seen what real conversations about the ways in which we approach problems or interact with our team can do, as long as they are genuine, nurture our unique essence, and empower us to build our capacity, to reach further than we thought possible. In these kinds of conversations, you can't give precise advice for how to color inside the lines, or even offer support for not thinking outside the box—you must abandon the lines and the box in search of something completely unknown.

Treating humans like complex beings living in a complex universe makes life more complicated. It requires taking the living systems perspective, in which we view everything as alive, evolving, and connected to everything else. Though challenging, seeing the world in this way is essential at this moment, when the challenges we face are both dire and brand new. Now we have to expand our ways of thinking, to look at an immediate challenge and attempt to see it within its greater context, to consider the ripple effects of each of our actions. By pushing against the edge again and again and turning possibilities into realities, we are taking steps now to live what we have the power to imagine. For this profound insight, I have Carol Sanford to thank.

Studying with Carol Sanford has blown my world wide open. She is a contrarian in the best sense of the word, someone totally unseduced by popular opinion or standard practice. As part of her regenerative business community, I am continually surprised to find that what I've always taken for granted as foundational isn't actually set in stone, that there is so much more complexity and potential in the world than I previously thought. This book isn't for those looking for a premade path; it's for anyone who is willing to take the more treacherous path of self-reflection and continual awakening, to find their own way by going within and seeing the world anew.

Sheryl O'Loughlin
CEO, REBBL Inc.,
Former CEO Clif Bar and Company,
Co-founder Plum Inc.
Executive Director of the Center for Entrepreneurial Studies,
Stanford Graduate School of Business

Preface

Why Critique the Most Popular Practice Ever? Toxicity!

I will admit from the start that this is a contrarian view of a subject that *I love to hate*: Feedback. People are often shocked that I would critique something that they think *must* be good for them and certainly good for others, no matter how much they dislike participating in it. After all, without feedback, how would we know how others see us? How would we get better at what we do?

My answer to this is that there is a much more effective way for people to accurately assess their work, improve their performance, and raise the level of their contributions—with none of the downsides or negative side effects of feedback.

If you are a manager or someone who supports managers, you are probably always seeking ways to help people succeed and to improve your organization. You might also want to make it possible for employees to appreciate their jobs and find work more meaningful. You may believe feedback is a great tool for getting this done. This book is written to show how it actually comes close to doing the exact opposite. I also hope to demonstrate that there is a far more effective way to get the results you are looking for and it is easier than you might think.

To accomplish this, I will relate a bit of feedback's history—how it was developed and sold to us as a *best practice*, how we were fooled into believing the pitch (it happened to all of us), and why we continue to miss the forest for the trees. More importantly, I will also show you why you cannot fix the feedback process by tweaking it, training people to do a better job of it, or hiring the right people for it in the first place. The problem is innate to the process itself.

While I want to make this lesson available to more people, I do not want you to adopt my thoughts or my truth. Instead, I offer ways for you to learn to deeply examine your own and others' ideas, to develop discernment, to think critically, and to take on change as a necessary and exhilarating aspect of human life. In order to clearly see the toxic nature of feedback, you will have to rigorously question my argument, reflect honestly on your own experience, and trust yourself to discern the truth. Our minds play tricks on us, and we will examine that phenomenon, too, because mind games lead us to believe in feedback. They will make it hard to let go, especially given our deep investment.

Be prepared to rethink your certainties and maybe even to forgive yourself along the way—and to forgive those who put you through craziness and exposed you to toxicity. I know this because it is what I had to do when I learned the truth about feedback. I had to forgive myself and forgive those who imposed it on me.

The good news is that my tested and proven alternative to feedback enables people to develop the clear thinking required to see themselves and their effects on others. This is a set of practices that empowers people to correct course, leap ahead, and perform better. An organization can function at its best without the corralling effect of feedback, and for that matter, without feedback's toxic companion practices. Those include performance reviews, discipline sessions, and plans for growth, to name just a few. Making people responsible for managing themselves does not require turning the asylum over to the inmates.

Here is a quick outline of the contents of this book.

- My own feedback story and how its effects on my well-being woke me up to feedback's toxicity, along with the research that put me back on the developmental path
- The higher aims of alternative practices that enable the development of three core capacities as a way to actually realize human potential
- A history of feedback that helps explain why organizations adopted it and how it became part of our educational institutions and businesses, and even most of our families as a tool for parenting
- A short lesson in psychology, discussing the deceptive ways in which the brain works to hide the harmful effects of feedback (and other toxic practices)
- A rundown of ways that feedback undermines the three core human capacities and causes many of the very problems it seeks to solve, including apathy, lack of initiative, and incomplete responsibility or self-centeredness
- Premises and principles to start you on the path to transformative human and business development, coupled with a list of resources to take you all the way if you choose
- Along the way, real-life examples of my work with companies that demonstrates both the negative effects of feedback and the potential of an alternative developmental path to produce growth transformation in any organization

Introduction

My Personal Experience with Feedback

My story is an overview of everything offered in this book. I wonder if it will feel familiar to you. Take notes! And be sure to let me know.

When I was almost 30 years old, I put myself on the track toward becoming a full university professor. I was working on a doctoral degree and teaching at San Jose State University in a combined program for graduate students in business, urban planning, and information technology (then called cybernetic systems). Each student earned a master's degree in one of these disciplines but took courses in all three.

Teaching and conducting research in the program exhilarated me, partly because I was the youngest member of an exceptionally experienced team of full professors. I did not mind being the kid on the block who often did the grunt work. Sadly, the program ended after only three years because a new dean of the business school chose to redistribute resources to other "worthier" endeavors. I had a dual master's in business and urban planning and was offered a teaching position in the Urban Planning Department. It was there that I experienced firsthand the devastating impact of what I had been teaching—ideas that were, in fact, toxic practices.

The Dean of Urban Planning fancied himself a great leader and coach of up-and-coming faculty. He was sincerely dedicated to this work, and he had an undergraduate minor in psychology that reinforced his confidence. He was introduced to feedback many years before, when he was in the military, and brought it with him to his new vocation.

After one month in my assistant professor role, I found myself sitting across from him wanting very much to be seen in a good light by my new superior. He held my future teaching career in his hands. He announced that I was going to be introduced to what he called a "cybernetic feedback method," one that we would recognize today as the forerunner of 360-degree feedback, which is conducted annually in many companies.

The dean gave me a form and explained that I was to evaluate myself against nine competencies defined by the faculty leadership team. I had seen these competencies before but was still a bit confused about how they applied to me and where I fit in their system. I did not expect that I also would be evaluated by my *peers*—a handful of faculty plus the chairman of the department. The dean was very patient with me. He answered all my questions and then set me off to come back the following week with my own evaluation. I was to receive the reflections of my peers within a month. The chairman would review these, add his own thoughts, and meet with me again within a couple of months.

I was surprised at the level of anxiety this process brought on in me—very surprised. At the time, I had been meditating for seven years, a practice that invites and supports looking at one's mind and its machinations. I was also part of a group that journaled together, using a set of practices that asked us to set personal aims (inner ones) based on learning and accomplishment (personal growth) objectives. We met monthly and used spiritual teachings as references. We did a lot of reflecting but never provided feedback to one another.

I did my feedback homework as required but I was pretty dissatisfied with the core competencies list as a reference against which to evaluate myself. Some competencies felt shallow or vague; for example, was I "able to listen and take criticism?" I wondered if that meant whether I was able to listen to all criticism and take all of it as useful. Some competencies seemed to be the opposite of what was most important to me as a faculty member. Analytical thinking was stressed but there was nothing on the systems thinking that was central to my work.

The competencies seemed academic to everyone I asked for help, and I got only very general ideas about how to apply them. Even the definitions and examples on the page of instructions were abstract. I attended a one-hour training where I watched a video on the process but that was no help either.

Even worse, a few of the competencies felt dead wrong. For example, one of the questions asked if I was "able to persuade and influence others." What had happened to co-create and collaborate? Neither was on the list, although there was a reference to teamwork. For the most part these questions, too, felt abstract and generic making it difficult to assess myself in a meaningful way. Equally important to me, not one of the nine competencies addressed how graduates from the department would successfully enter the real world, given our contributions to their learning.

Truly, everything that I felt was really great and challenging about teaching did not appear on this list—namely, the ability to make sense out of very complicated ideas and engage others in understanding them together. Developing this competency was the very reason I had asked to be part of the cross-discipline teaching team in the program that had been shut down. Here, in my new position, it did not seem to count at all.

The people evaluating me were a mix of those I had worked with, even if not closely, and others who knew me from a bit of distance. I taught department courses on social and psychological aspects of communities while working on my doctorate in cognitive and organization psychology. My dissertation research examined how researchers almost always (consciously or unconsciously) influenced their research hypothesis, methodology, execution, and findings.

The method for my own research was to ask researchers to assess themselves using a journaling process and then to engage them in an interview about their findings. (I followed up with half of them a few years later and found that what they had learned about themselves working with me on this project continued to guide their self-directed development and professional work.) I started this research when I was teaching in the cross-degree program and carried it forward in the Urban Planning Department. Within the context of my meditation practice, journaling group, and research, I also journaled my experiences, interior and exterior, working on the feedback form required by my new position.

My peers offered many ideas intended to help me grow. For example, their comments included, "Spend more time writing out your lectures so that less is left to chance and your presentations are not incomplete. This should enable you or others to replicate your lectures for classes in the future." Most of these faculty knew or had heard that I favored working from outlines of key points. I used the life situations of my students, in real time in the class, to teach principles based on their actual organization and community experience. This was intended to draw out what they had learned and rigorously test my own ideas. It worked so well and generated such enthusiastic learning that I and my students often ended up staying after class for more conversation and exploration.

To my peers, this did not seem to match the competency to "be well prepared and able to benchmark thoroughness and repeatability." The department chairman gave these remarks to me and added another suggestion: I was to learn to "simplify core concepts and require less effort from students to extract them, in order to prevent confusion and lack of clarity concerning what the test will include." But, unbeknownst to my chairman, I did not test my students. I assigned them to develop projects that would create real change and then to write papers developing a theory of change based on their concrete experiences carrying out their projects. This was a graduate program. Was I really supposed to be spoon-feeding information to my students?

The outcome of my feedback process was two objectives, which were written into my development plan: 1) simplify my course and make what I wanted students to learn more explicit from the beginning, and 2) write out my lectures to make them more thorough and repeatable in order to ensure transference. I was given training assignments and quarterly benchmarks to follow up on. I mark this as the first day of a two-year period during which I mostly stopped listening to myself and gave up ways of working based on what I knew, deep down, to be far better. Looking back, this seems almost inevitable. It was a pattern carried forward from my childhood. Feedback had hit me in one of my most vulnerable places.

And this pattern was ingrained not just in me. I recognized from my own research that it commonly developed from the way most children are raised in Western society. I also had seen it in an experimental research project I conducted that demonstrated how easy it is to get children to abandon their own ideas and focus on what adults or powerful others want them to do and think. I knew this was behavior built into our brains. We all need to belong; the fear of being ostracized is part of our survival instinct. This instinct is so powerful that it causes children to lie to themselves and others about what they are doing. Instead, they mirror what others tell them they ought to be doing—or, if they do not lie, they experience painful doubt about themselves and their own ways of thinking.

Aspiring to become a full professor in a cross-discipline program meant I needed to learn to function in an environment where others were part of a process that taught us how to see ourselves. At the one-year feedback follow-up, I was considered to have improved on both fronts. I had worked hard in this new direction and taken my training seriously. But I was still keeping my journal, consistently recording feelings that what I was asked to do was not serving my students well. I taught differently, and I was perceived to be better at it. But my newly developed capabilities and the method of working I was developing did not fit me or my teaching philosophy at all. They adhered to supposedly core competencies, and yet I felt that the objectives in my development plan came from the ideas of other people about what good teaching at the graduate level looked like. In their earnest attempts to help me grow, my peers judged me against their own shortfalls and well-intentioned preconceptions.

I left San Jose State one year later, feeling that I could no longer enjoy a work track that required me to sacrifice the real value I had to offer students and what they most needed from their graduate programs. I wanted to work with the Socratic method on very complex subjects. I wanted to engage with people in organization and community leadership roles on work that would enable them to discern paths forward through complex and extraordinarily challenging situations. I soon came to understand my disappointing experience in the Urban Planning Department as a conflict of epistemology, defined as how people learn and the acceptable means of helping them come to know something.

It took me about five years to find a different, truer path to what I wanted to accomplish. The alternatives that I created to replace toxic practices such as 360-degree feedback are the result of that search. I began to develop them when I finally learned to trust myself, to know and work from *my* essence, and to listen to *my* ideas. This life change enabled me to find teachers and colleagues who thought that what I did was amazing and wanted to learn how to do it for themselves—not merely to imitate what I did. These people were passionately committed to finding and following their own paths to innovation, based on discovery of their own essences and ideas.

The biggest surprise of this transition was that I discovered how many people had stopped listening to themselves, and were keeping their heads down and working within the system. I was also surprised by the strength of their hope and desire to find ways to fulfill their potential in the professional worlds they had worked so hard to enter. Some had left their institutions in search of a different path, as I had. Some had stayed and made their way as best they could. Often they had given up. They had come to believe the toxic stories told to them in feedback sessions. If they had managed to stop dwelling on them, they were nevertheless mostly silenced, and their original dreams were obscured.

I felt deeply that I wanted to help those who had not found ways to be fully themselves in professional environments. By the time I was 35, I had focused on businesses, particularly corporations, as the places I thought I might be able to succeed in carrying out this personal mission. These were the organizations where most people made their livings, and where large groups of people had to adhere to guidelines and programs over which they had little or no control. I soon found a way to create evolutionary changes in business practice, based on the ideas I had about how organizations could work for the benefit of all—customers, employees and cocreators, communities, ecosystems, and stockholders—in other words, the people I now refer to collectively as "stakeholders."

The door to this way forward was opened through a set of conversations with managers who knew that something was wrong and wanted help. A wide gap existed between what they thought were the sources of their challenges and what I knew they had not yet learned to see. To me, this was my great opportunity to contribute to the world, and it was where I began the next stage of my professional development. I grabbed it and I am still running with it.

PART ONE

A TECHNOLOGY OF CHANGE

CHAPTER 1

FIVE CHALLENGES TO DISCERNMENT

Why is it that organizational leaders, and people in general, have such difficulty recognizing the negative impacts of their business practices and work designs? Why do we so deeply believe in what is later found to be not only untrue but often harmful? What allowed me, as a young assistant professor with high aspirations, to give in to 360-degree feedback?

FALSE CERTAINTIES ARE NOT MY FAULT—OR YOURS!

Do you remember the low-fat craze? I do. I put on about 30 pounds before I lost faith in my low-fat diet. Not that I blamed the regime. I followed it erratically, off it as often as I was on. I did not question its premise and kept eating the low-fat way for decades, undermining my health even as I studied and debunked misguided business practices. My unexamined eating habits led to diabetes and high blood pressure. When I finally heard the messages my body was sending and realized I had fallen for false research, I felt really stupid for a long time. I had been duped by claims concocted by industries pushing harmful products to make money.

We do not need to go into the details of that fiasco but we do need to understand how it was possible and why so many smart people were taken in, including me. At this stage of life, I consider myself to be intelligent, highly discerning, and conscious that my choices are my own. But I still get mad at myself for falling victim to the low-fat scam.

Developing this kind of understanding—in this instance, by tackling feedback—is an invitation to engage in a process of discernment that is extremely difficult, even for those with the best of intentions. Real blinders prevent us from seeing how we were sold a bill of goods and defended it. I have come to define them as the five big challenges or restraints of which we are mostly unaware, especially if we are not thinking critically about ourselves and others. I still have to remind myself of these challenges, and I am someone who writes and teaches about them every day of my life!

The Challenges

FIRST, WE ARE CULTURALLY DEPENDENT. That is, all of us live in a culture interwoven with what social psychologists call "implicit agreements." To belong and be accepted by our communities, we agree to accept the dominant patterns governing our way of interpreting and making sense of events. These patterns seem right to us; we do not question them. They often include our political and religious leanings, our understanding of how relationships work, what makes for success, and how we view ourselves within our families. So many people with power and influence tell us these agreements are true, that it is hard to go against the grain and question them. And if we did, we might well be ostracized by groups of people we depend on for our well-being (family, friends, teachers, colleagues, congregations, agencies), which would leave us feeling alone, unstable, unloved, and alienated.

SECOND, THERE IS NO PROCESS READILY AVAILABLE TO MOST OF US FOR QUESTIONING THE ASSUMPTIONS AND AGREEMENTS THAT HAVE SHAPED US. Most communities never question or invite individuals to question what they have been taught their whole lives by their families, schools, employers, religious communities, and social circles. What everyone thinks and believes is so familiar (and the brain loves what is familiar) that it seems sacrilegious and cynical to question anything. "Better not!" our society seems to say.

Third, like bees seeking nectar, the human brain seeks and adheres to what is familiar. This statement is related to the idea that all people hate change. For the most part, we have to be taught to value and take charge of discerning and enacting beneficial change. However, we are disadvantaged by the oldest part of the human brain, the function that evolved to issue alerts when we are unsafe, likely to be attacked by a tiger or some other enemy, which is always triggered by what is unfamiliar. At the least hint that something near us has been altered, the fight or flight response kicks in, flooding our bodies with cortisol and then adrenaline, and producing a mental suspicion that the new thing will undermine our safety and success. I define this fear as *the inability to know how to relate to what has changed*. We refer casually to its mental consequences as a "meltdown."

Fear of change kicks in even when people are faced with life-threatening risks that require immediate changes in behavior. Studies reveal that when patients with heart disease who have undergone traumatic bypass surgery are told that, unless they adjust their lifestyle, they will quickly die, only about 9 percent are able to change their old behaviors. We see something like this every day in organizations undergoing change. Mount Eliza Business School researched change initiatives in companies and found that more than 70 percent fail—not because they are not sound business ideas but because people resist them in order to avoid change.

The trick to changing our behavior is to change what we mistakenly think we are seeing and thinking but this is difficult largely because human brains are extremely effective and tenacious in maintaining the status quo. The good news is that—balancing this rather primitive mechanism of resistance—our brain cells are continually forming new connections and restructuring our perceptions and physiology. This process of neuroplasticity happens thousands of times a day and gives us enormous potential to change, individually and collectively, if only we can find and learn to manage the sources of resistance. But we need help. Speaking of which…

FOURTH, MOST OF US DO NOT HAVE ACCESS TO COMMUNITIES THAT CAN EFFECTIVELY SUPPORT US AS WE LEARN TO MANAGE CHANGE. We can do this work only with the help of people who accept and regularly initiate change and consider this to be a natural and *happy* part of life. These people—who I call *resources*—are most often found in organizations and communities where change is considered normal and valued, and where individuals are ostracized only when they refuse to develop discernment and the willingness to change. Resources help us engage in rigorous questioning and reflection as part of developmental processes that are available to everyone.

FIFTH, MOST OF US ALSO DO NOT HAVE ACCESS TO THE NECESSARY TECHNOLOGY FOR ADDRESSING THESE CHALLENGES. In any creative field, people need technologies, vocabularies, frameworks, and ways of engaging in community to develop their highest levels of capability. This is as true of businesspeople as it is of screenwriters, plumbers, and attorneys. All jobs worth doing require apprenticeship and often extensive formal education before practitioners qualify to become journeymen and then move up to leadership positions. No one can succeed without a well-tested and validated technology and the capability to use it.

The developmental alternatives to feedback and other toxic practices are instruments in a larger technology of change that provides ways of dealing with each of these five limitations, rather than seeking detours around them and causing potentially even worse problems.

THE BEGINNING OF CHANGE

When I first enter any company, no matter how large or small, new or established, I get the same questions. Every executive, without exception, asks some version of, "What do you do with people who do not want to change, people who do not take initiative, who wait to be told what to do before they act?"

It does little good in a first meeting to respond that it is them and their work practices that create and perpetuate the passivity disabling their organizations. I know without asking that they have embraced one or more of the hundred toxic practices in existence, nearly one-third of which I briefly described in my book, *The Regenerative Business.*[1]

Of these practices, feedback is one of the most counterproductive and widespread.

Another question that I am often asked is, "What have you found in your forty years' experience that predictably produces a successful business and workforce?" This question is the same as the questions, "What makes democracies work?" and "What enables people to contribute to their full potential?" An honest effort to answer will follow the same thread and arrive at the same basic conclusion about human development: Success of any kind arises from the ability we all share to develop *three core capacities,* and our willingness to design work systems and practices that support their development and foster them in our culture.

The technology of change that I am offering here is a method for thinking and developing as a human with fully realized core capacities. This is the only practical route to developing facility with discernment and change, and it is a far better route than feedback for nurturing conscious employees.

I am willing to bet that most of my readers were never taught that this technology exists or that it is one they need to learn. We rarely see people around us practicing it, and unless you grew up in a traditional native society or got a solid education in Western or Eastern classics, you never truly learned how to become a discerning human being.

Chapter 2

Three Core Human Capacities

All people have far more potential than they achieve in their short lives. This is partly because we do not know how to properly support human growth and development. In fact, we do not know the foundational capacities that, if fully developed, would give people the extraordinary ability to grow themselves and contribute to the growth of everyone around them. Developing these capacities also would engender more courage and vision.

For the most part, we work on the wrong things, such as the nine competencies I was asked to take on at San Jose State. Those particular proficiencies had little to do with producing good urban planners, let alone fulfilled and creative students, employees, or citizens. Because we do not work directly on the underlying capacities necessary to achieve worthwhile aims, we undermine their realization. This is what I mean by toxic practices. These ways of working are lethal to the foundational capacities that make us fully ourselves and provide springboards for great lives, allowing us to achieve our full potential and make beneficial contributions to others.

The journaling and meditation I practiced as a graduate student, and the small community I shared them with, were based in ancient wisdom teachings that evolved in many cultures, Western and Eastern. I have carried these practices and teachings with me through my entire life, and from them I developed understanding of the three core human capacities, which that I will share with you now. Although I was a long way from articulating them at the time, I could feel these capacities working in me when I left San Jose State to carry on my research. I expect that many of my readers here are familiar with them in one form or another, and that all of you feel them working in you or you would not have stayed with me to this moment in the feedback story.

The three core human capacities are *locus of control, scope of considering,* and *source of agency.* They are innate in all people but most of our societal roles offer few opportunities to develop them.[2]

This leaves many of us with only rudimentary or accidentally developed awareness of them and little readiness to call on them. It also limits the range of our life experiences and our ability to advance into ever more responsible roles in our families, organizations, and communities.

THREE CORE CAPACITIES

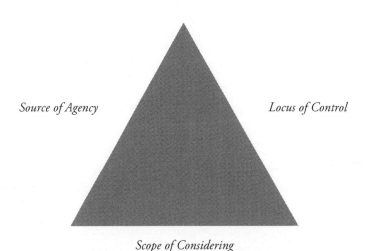

Source of Agency

Locus of Control

Scope of Considering

Locus of control speaks to the degree to which we experience and exercise control over our own lives, particularly on the direction of our self-development and our resilience to adversity. The second leg of the triad, scope of considering, relates to what we take into account in our actions and endeavors, especially in relation to other people and living beings. We may be self-centered and inwardly focused, or we may consider the effects of our actions on other individuals and groups or entire living systems. The difference is between a *self-centered* focus on oneself alone and a *systems-actualizing* focus on evolving a larger whole—marriage, family, organization, community, industry, ecosystem, planet—in order to create beneficial changes.

Source of agency refers to where we find authority for our initiative or actions. We may rely almost exclusively on the authority of others to direct us or we may have within us the will to initiate action ourselves and follow through with self-directed efforts. The more we are able to direct ourselves, the better our capability is to connect to larger systems and help actualize them.

The degree to which any of the three capacities has been developed in given individuals can be roughly located on a spectrum. Locus of control moves from external, seeing our lives as determined by others, to internal, taking accountability for what we exercise in terms of outcomes and level of direction. We are able to go back and forth between external and internal but we have usually settled into a tendency toward one or the other by the time we reach adulthood.

Scope of considering is in a sense the opportunity to get perspective on the internal and external events of our lives. When we consider only ourselves (*internal considering*), every situation we encounter is all about us. The whole world revolves around us. On the other hand, if we are sensitive to others in our world and to other forms of life, we have developed a degree of *external considering*. As with locus of control, we can be on either end of the spectrum or anywhere between, and we may be more or less able to be where we want all of the time. None of us has constancy in the continuum but each of us has a tendency toward one end of the spectrum or the other.

Source of agency is likewise very fluid but tends to be directed by beliefs we hold about our roles in the world and who has power or influence over us. When we live according to an authoritarian worldview, we often wait for important others to activate, or direct, or stop us. But as we become driven internally and come to believe that the world is ours, we begin to move toward a life devoted to stepping up and making a difference. We develop *personal agency*, the courage to demand more of ourselves and respond to internal calls that connect us to powerful opportunities. Yet again, like locus of control and scope of considering, this source is not constant but moves on a continuum from self-centered to systems actualizing.

Without conscious development, these three core capacities may stay nascent our entire lives, diminishing us and limiting the contribution we can make. But if we are willing to develop them by ourselves or hand-in-hand with organizations or communities designed to work on such development, we may be astounded by how much we can grow and how fully ourselves we can become. The challenge is to avoid the practices and systems that steer us toward a smaller perspective and set of pursuits.

An Exercise: Self-Centered or Systems Actualizing?

Engaging in a short, reflective exercise can help make sense of these ideas. It is especially helpful to return to its questions over the course of a month or two and to share your reflections with one or two other people. This will lead to deeper insights and discoveries and may even result in useful applications for real-life situations. Start by taking each capacity in turn and reflecting on how it shows up in your own life (or does not).

Internal locus of control is the certainty that responsibility for any and all outcomes rests with oneself. A person cannot control everything that happens around or within them, but they can take responsibility for their reactions and self-development in the midst of it all.

For a person with well-developed internal locus of control, losing a job or ending a marriage becomes an opportunity to rethink life. Research shows that people with this capacity do a better job of personal financial planning than those who do not have it. They are healthier and more productive. They are far happier, too, even in the face of life's most unnerving or threatening challenges.

External locus of control, the opposite of internal locus of control, presents itself as passivity and victimhood, blaming others for our shortfalls and difficulties, and finding excuses for not delivering on promises. Although we are all more or less able in any moment to act from internal locus of control, people for whom external locus of control is mostly constant cannot be counted on. They let us down. They do not step up. They are hard to be around in most life situations. Of course, this does not mean that they cannot change, only that, like most of the rest of us, they have not had opportunities to become more self-aware. This realization alone can give us the impetus to explore ways to develop awareness in ourselves and our organizations.

Where does locus of control show up for you as the feeling that you are accountable for your actions and for your reactions to the actions of others? Where do you shun responsibility and fall into blaming others, imagining that you are the victim of their actions?

Think about yesterday. Where were you on the scale below?

EXTERNAL CONSIDERING, as it is called in most philosophical texts, is exercising our connection to others, not being concerned about only ourselves. It is the source of charity and generosity, but it is also dedication to educating others and being of service to them in their efforts to develop character, confidence, and perseverance. When external considering is missing, selfishness is the primary way of being. All actions and changes are valued only in terms of how they will affect "me, personally" and bring me benefits. Those who are not practicing external considering may give others the sensation that they are unseen and unheard, pawns in a bureaucratic game, treated as if they were not fully alive. The tragedy of our time is that we have not understood that; like external locus of control, this can be remedied by the practice of self-observation and self-reflection.

When in your life do you make decisions based primarily on what's best for you and those closest to you? Why is it appropriate to go beyond consideration of yourself and your loved ones to others who are not so close? How might you do this more often? Are there times when you might significantly expand your consideration to include the impact of your decisions and actions on people you do not usually take into account? When do you begin to include a neighboring community, a social system, or the ecosystem in which you dwell?

When is it meaningful to think of taking on the evolution of a system that may be underserving many people because it is not realizing its highest potential? As an example, reflect on the inequity of the criminal justice system, although it may not necessarily be causing you personal harm. Making beneficial changes to this system—reforming it to serve all people at an equally high level of fairness—is what I would call "systems actualizing."

Think again about yesterday. With your answers to these questions in mind, ask yourself where you were on the scale below.

Self-Centered   **Systems Actualizing**

Internal   External

SCOPE OF CONSIDERING

Personal agency is the effective exercise of the will to act and make chang-es that benefit ourselves and others. It is the opposite of the passivity that executives complain so much about in their workers. When fully developed, personal agency transforms individuals into leaders, go-getters, and change agents. People acting from personal agency notice what goes on around them and respond to what is less than optimal or just plain wrong. They cannot tolerate sitting passively by when what is failing is not confronted or put right. The opposite of this kind of person is one who will work responsibly but usually only when someone whose authority they respect or fear dictates exactly what must be done. The difference between the two is easily seen as the difference between willingness to take risks and avoid them.

When you are called to make decisions or to take action, do you locate authority in yourself or in others? When do you ignore things that could be improved because they do not impact you negatively? When do you let your-self be influenced by those with authority, for fear of ruffling feathers? Are there places where you might make needed change if you activated yourself to care more deeply or to face up to your own fears or distractions? We often allow ourselves to be swayed by the opinions or advice of others, primarily to protect our prestige, position, or role. What or whom do you allow to influence your decisions to exercise your agency or not?

With your reflections on these questions in mind, ask yourself where you were yesterday on the scale below.

FURTHER REFLECTIONS involve assessing the possible impacts of self-centeredness and system actualization on your professional practice, business, or organization. Take one capacity at a time—locus of control, scope of considering, and source of agency—and reflect on the following questions:

1. What difference does your tendency toward one end of the spectrum or the other make in your work life? Or in other aspects of your life?

2. What happens to an organization whose culture pulls people to one end or the other? How does that affect the meaning people find in their roles or their impacts on other stakeholders (e.g. customers or students)? How does it impact the organization as a good place to work? Or financially?

3. How do your own work design and practices play into this? What do you find when you take one practice at a time and reflect on its impact?

Perfecting the core capacities is never possible because they are inexhaustible. All of us will move back and forth on the scales from moment to moment throughout each day. The important question in any moment is, "Which way am I moving?" When we are able to return to ourselves and take note of where we are, we also can ask, "Would other options serve the development and expression of these capacities in a more complete way?" Recall this exercise and these questions as you move forward with Chapter 3, looking at ways to design work and work practices that develop the core human capacities.

CHAPTER 3

LOOKING AHEAD:
ALTERNATIVES TO FEEDBACK AND
OTHER TOXIC PRACTICES

The exercise above may have given you a sense of your own inner organization and your current place on the path toward fully realizing your capacity. The key to further development is to stay tuned in to your constant back-and-forth movement on the three scales. The alternatives to toxic practices and systems are all based on the ability to engage in self-reflection, which becomes more accurate, motivational, and innovative when development of the three capacities is remembered as an ultimate aim.

WHAT CAN WE DO INSTEAD?

What if people could see themselves and their behaviors so clearly that no feedback or other assistance was needed to guide them in their work? When self-observation and reflection are consistently tied to what I call "Big Promises" to stakeholders, better, more compelling motives are the natural result. When we ask ourselves about the difference we are making in other people's lives, we cannot help but be moved to think more creatively, to do more and do it better. It is a matter of asking questions like, "How am I changing my customer or my consumer's life? Am I doing it well? Where do I need to be more ambitious and innovative for them?"

My own experience as a graduate student made it abundantly clear that this is not only possible but also preferable. What if we primarily taught people to engage in self-reflection, self-direction, and self-management of their own growth and development? What if we asked them to play more powerful roles and to be part of growing one another's capacities in work that required no outside feedback or input?

After I left my position at San Jose State, I decided to run a short research project to test the idea that *not* telling people what to work on in themselves is a better way to support changes in behavior than feedback. This meant not sharing ideas or opinions about the possible effects their changes might have on others or on their work—and not even hinting what they might work on.

I knew a teacher at an elementary school in Honesdale, Penn., and asked her if together we could do a short experiment with some of her third-grade students—all boys, as it turned out. Eighteen sets of parents gave permission, thinking it might help them learn how to be better at raising their children. They understood our protocol and trusted the teacher, and me, by extension.

All of the students were part of a larger group participating in a school-wide program to teach them about values of honesty and respect. (At the time, lack of these values seemed to be widespread throughout the United States, which had triggered programs like this one in many schools.) Faculty said that young children were having trouble seeing and telling the truth, even in objective observation activities. There was no evidence that this was any more prevalent than in the past but people felt it should be addressed.

For my study, we split 18 boys into two equal groups—one traditional control group and another experiment group. We set up a one-way window through which I and a couple of colleagues could observe each group as they were guided by proctors through a challenging activity. My colleagues were there as a part of the protocol that I had devised to remove my own bias from observations. I did not share my hypothesis with them or the students, and only the parents and teacher knew what I was testing for. Everyone else had to wait to hear the outcomes.

My protocol was simple. It included an observable activity in which proctors asked students to raise their hands in a set pattern on the count of one to five. They were to adjust the positions of their arms only when the number was called and they were asked to move. In between movements, they were to remain still. The proctors conducted the activity with each group separately.

After the first round of the activity, the proctors asked each group separately to say how they had done at moving only when prompted and positioning their hands correctly. Not one boy in either group was even close to the right timing or placement, but both groups responded positively, claiming to have performed the activity successfully. After this first round of reflection, the proctors changed the movement and timing protocol for each group, and then led them through the activity a second time.

CONTROL GROUP: Proctors then asked the control group if they would like to see a video of their activity to help them reflect on and assess their success the second time. With blank faces, the proctors set up the video. The students watched, a bit stunned to see that their arms were all over the place, rarely in the right positions. When the proctors gently asked if seeing the video changed their minds about how they had done, not one of them spoke.

The proctors next asked the control group to do the activity a third time, using exactly the same protocol as they had the second time. The boys made no improvement as they went through the activity. When they were asked again to evaluate their success, they were less vocal and a bit more cautious, but they expressed belief that they had done well by shaking their heads in response to questions. Again, the proctors offered to show them a video recording of the activity as they had just performed it. After viewing the video, they were asked if they wanted to change their minds about how they had done. This time, they offered no real reaction at all.

We observed that on this third time around, students did a lot of watching one another. When asked if they wanted to see the video, most said yes. Afterward, they were silent, and no one responded when they were asked for their reaction to the video.

EXPERIMENT GROUP: With the experiment group, the proctors conducted the second round of the activity the same way they had the first. They asked the students to evaluate their success and got the same affirmation that they had done well. But instead of asking them if they wanted to see a video, the proctors asked, "How would you do it better next time?" The students' reaction indicated clearly that they had not expected the question. They were silent for a moment, and then they suggested doing it over again more slowly.

The proctors obliged, and the third time the group did the activity, they counted at a pace half as fast as in the first two rounds. There was clearly an improved ability to follow the steps with better timing and placement of arms relative to the prescribed position. Still, no one in the group did the activity successfully.

The proctors asked, "How would you do it even better next time?" This time the students were ready with ideas. The next time they performed the activity, they asked to stand in front of the large mirror in the room (which was used as a ballet studio at other times) and to stand in a line, rather than in the circle they had adopted the second time around. Once again, they got better at moving their hands in time with the count.

In the fifth and final run through, the students suggested changing the instructions to make them harder. They instructed the proctors to count to 10 and to assign different positions. This time, all the students performed amazingly well, following the timing and placing their hands precisely in the prescribed positions. They had set the challenge themselves, and they rose to it.

OBSERVATIONS: I made several observations when I published my research. First, the students did a better job when they felt they had an opportunity to improve and were not stuck with a single inflexible protocol. Second, given the chance, they pushed their own boundaries by taking on a harder challenge. Third, they cooperated with each other more successfully when they were not shown the video—that is, when they did not feel that they could be caught doing something they were not supposed to be doing. Fourth, after the first invitation to offer suggestions, their personal agency emerged. They began to initiate improvements, and they gave the proctors instructions on how to guide them. And fifth, they were willing to tell the truth about how well they performed the activity when they trusted that they would not be judged or shamed for their failures.

But the most amazing thing occurred when we went back to the control group and repeated the experiment group's protocol with them, asking them to go through the same set of steps each time, showing no videos, and giving them an opportunity to suggest ways to improve their performance. Although their ideas for improvement were different, they improved their work, made it more complicated, and experienced the same rise in personal agency. And they accomplished this in one afternoon—from confidence to deflation to amazing success. The deflation did not seem to affect their potential for success. They recovered and went on to succeed without missing a beat.

One footnote: All of the teachers at the school asked to learn more about the self-directed development technology, a tiny fraction of which we had used in our research with the third-grade boys. We shared it with them, and it spread to other schools in Honesdale.

From this initial study, it seemed to me that the drive to be self-regulating, self-improving, and self-challenging is innate in all of us and ready to be tapped. I did a few additional bits of research on the idea later with adults in work settings. Each time, results confirmed what I had observed as a young instructor: Put a person in charge of their own assessment, and they will soar.

I went on to figure out how to do this kind of exercise in businesses, and I found that the protocol perfectly paralleled my experience with the elementary school students. I also discovered many more toxic practices, and externally guided and evaluated activities, which moved people away from the three core human capacities. For most people I met, these repeated patterns that they had experienced throughout their lives. I found that I could awaken their core capacities and bring them to life in a very short time by switching to work designs based on self-regulation, self-direction, and self-motivation in the form of Big Promises.

The hurdle at the beginning of each change process was encouraging organization leaders in charge of toxic practices and programs to let go of the old patterns. They were attached to the familiar routines and defensive about losing them, clinging to the idea that what they had perpetuated remained the correct course. Their brains were prompting them to seek the safety of tradition and cultural agreement.

Moving leaders—and businesspeople, generally—to try on new ways of thinking was much like working with the students in my primary school research groups. The same principles applied to initiating their self-directed change: Start with and maintain a structured educational process based on developing the three core human capacities. Put people in charge of their own change in collaboration with others. Provide them with guardrails in the form of a strategic business direction. Ask good questions (with no attachment to correct answers) to open the way for them to design their own individual and team evolution, always using the educational process as the springboard for innovation.

———————

There is much more to say about developmental practices, including:

- What are the guardrails for development and how do they work?
- What are our working premises and principles and how do we validate them?
- How do we develop the capacity in people to work developmentally?
- How do we build a culture to support this way of working, one in which reflection and assessment come from ourselves and not from others?
- How do we purge all of our assessment processes of the biases and attachments that make feedback so toxic?

Before we answer these questions, it is important to understand how old, familiar practices stand in the way of transitions to greater responsibility, happier people, and higher levels of productivity and profitability. It starts with feedback.

Part Two

Feedback

Chapter 4

What Is Feedback?

In terms of human methodologies, feedback is *offering or receiving opinions, impressions, and assessments of attitudes and behavior from others in any form or context*. Feedback is based on the ideas that: 1) people cannot see themselves clearly and cannot objectively assess the effects of their actions, and 2) external observers—assumed to be clear-eyed, unprejudiced, and reliably objective—must do this work for them. Feedback is given with the intention of helping others change their behaviors in ways that will benefit their work teams and organizations. Its primary goal is to improve performance reviews, teamwork engagements, and people's ability to align themselves with business strategies and objectives.

With this definition and an understanding of the core human capacities as guides, we are ready to look at the history of feedback with three objectives in mind:

1. To see why resourcing development of the three core capacities may be the most important and generous gift one can give to another person
2. To become familiar with some powerful practices that accomplish the desirable outcomes we rarely see feedback deliver: improvements in people's capability to observe and direct themselves, to make bigger contributions to the business and its customers, and to become ever more resilient in the face of criticism and setbacks

3. To understand why innovation is possible only when an entire organization is engaged in Big Promises based on a strategic direction,
and to understand that feedback and other limiting practices are the
surest way to discourage the development of capacities that makes
these promises possible

The most important objective is the first one. Giving people what they need
to observe and manage their own behaviors, and to initiate actions from
within themselves is how we develop the three human capacities. This is the
most important work we can do for another human being. Further, I hope to
make it evident that feedback not only slows down this development, it may
also completely derail it—either temporarily, which was my experience at
San Jose State, or permanently, as has sadly been the case for others.

My experience and research show that these effects occur no matter how well
feedback is practiced, regardless of training and preparation or good intentions (which is also true for other toxic practices). Input from other people
tends to trigger our need to belong, a response demanded by our brain for
survival. This causes us to give external input more weight than our own reflections, which encourages us to work toward others' ideas and suggestions
instead of toward our own. Over time, we become dependent on input from
outside ourselves. It becomes our default for confirmation and motivation,
and it can happen to anyone, from children in school with teachers and peers
to adults with personal and professional relationships.

More importantly, feedback undermines and erodes our capacity for self-reflection and self-direction. This is true even of people who loudly proclaim
the good feedback does them by providing information they never would
have uncovered on their own. This kind of declaration is often motivated by
a push from the brain to establish belonging. It is often heartfelt and sincere
but not nearly as powerful as the thrill of self-discovery.

Defense of feedback is also sometimes motivated by attachment to something that is better than the really bad stuff. By "really bad stuff" I mean
encounters with others who tell you exactly what they think of you, evaluat-

ing you based only on their privately held thoughts, which can seem terribly biased and strand you with no positive way forward. No one wants this. Feedback has got to be better because it is conducted according to a process that requires at least some attempt at objectivity, by a group of peers or a supervisor with some stake in keeping you productive. But maybe not. As Nobel Laureate economist Herbert A. Simon says, "Attachment to the better is the enemy of the best."

In another twist on the bad-better-best case, the prevailing idea that it is always better to get the real truth about yourself from someone else, someone with an objective eye, has limited people's ability to independently develop their sense of self. People are discouraged before they even begin the destabilizing yet thoroughly rewarding effort of finding their truth for themselves. Every one of us can learn to observe ourselves, reflect on what we see, and develop deep insights into our thinking, feelings, and behaviors. We can do a much better job of that than others can do for us. In doing so, we develop capabilities that serve us well in all of our endeavors and afford us a great sense of fulfillment and personal development.

In a business, developing the capability to be self-observing and self-reflective must be coupled with turning everyone's minds outward to the effects they have on market forces, particularly on their customers and consumers. Those who are responsible for providing new levels of services and products must make direct contact with customers in order to understand their aspirations and what can help them achieve them. For this, it does no good to rely on customer feedback. Only direct contact can be the source of new ideas, and the energy and excitement to deliver them. It fosters strong interest and commitment to customers' successes. And this is equally true for all other stakeholders, including cocreators, stockholders, communities, and ecosystems.

As it turns out, trying to think for other people weakens them by undermining the development of their own capability to be self-observing and self-directed. External input tends to shut down the growth and exercise of personal agency, respect and appreciation for the contributions of others, and belief in our responsibility for what goes on around us or happens to us. Feedback poses several specific problems, which we will examine separately and then in terms of their cumulative effects; it is the least likely way of changing other people's attitudes and behaviors.

Of course, feedback is widespread and often revered as a best practice. There are no universal criteria for best practices. Nevertheless, it is assumed as one and utilized directly by 90 percent of organizations under the mistaken belief that it will improve the performance of all workers, whether presented in the form of criticism or praise. As we will see, this is simply not the case. The benefits of feedback are purely mythological.

Let's pause a moment here to draw a distinction. It is not a question of whether feedback works. It does! The need to belong will drive changes in behavior whether they are in line with people's intentions or not, as shown by my personal experience with feedback. The real questions are: Does feedback encourage and make it possible for all people to develop the three core human capacities—locus of control, scope of considering, and source of agency—which drives our ableness to live fully in the world and take action? Do the changes offered by feedback shoot too low—even when they exceed the downright bad and the only fairly decent? And, can we see higher possibilities and make the necessary changes in our organizations to realize them? I know that we can because I have witnessed businesses and other organizations do it time and again.

LESSONS LEARNED THE HARD WAY

To make the changes necessary for a business to serve all of its stakeholders well, it is of utmost importance that its leaders ask themselves some tough questions. For example:

- In my experience, have people seemed slow to change as the result of our feedback processes? Or, have they been changing quickly but apparently without examining what the change might mean for them?
- Do some people seem never to change much at all?
- Do people seem distracted or anxious in the periods leading up to feedback sessions, either because they will be called on to give it or because they will receive it?
- Have I ever suspected that an unexamined judgment (positive or negative) has coalesced around an individual's behavior and is showing up inappropriately in feedback?
- Do our feedback processes often leave people feeling isolated?
- Are people forming cliques to support one another that detract from the team effort?

These sample questions describe only a few of the hundreds of possible experiences that indicate how, despite good intentions and regular upgrades, a feedback program inevitably will not deliver the expected benefits.

Sometimes that experience may be extreme, such as when I was called in as an educator to Weyerhaeuser, one of the world's largest private owners of timberlands, at one of their pulping operations in New Bern, N.C. The company's business leaders had initiated a performance-enhancing feedback process, in which managers gave one another feedback along with their supervisors. They had been trained to do this in a way that was more productive and more sensitive than past versions of the program. Feedback sessions for each manager were preceded by written evaluations by the supervisor and other managers, which were then aggregated into a summary before being presented to the manager. All identifying characteristics of the writers were removed to focus attention on the information versus the people who offered it. This process took place over several months and culminated with a meeting between each manager and their supervisor to create a performance improvement plan based on the total feedback.

I remember very well a manager named Jerry, who had been at the facility for 14 years and was assigned a role in production oversight. He saw general managers come and go, as well as some turnover among his peers. His was a high performing team in terms of results but it operated very differently than others in the facility. He was highly participative in the work and encouraged a lot of discussion at team meetings.

Jerry was a skeptic by nature—not because he didn't trust people but because he had come to believe that a person's initial thinking is automatic and not . . . well, not thoughtful. He was not a cynic or argumentative but he did question things a lot. Why were things done the way they were? What did this comment from someone really mean? His questions covered everything from accounting forms he was required to complete to strategic decisions he was expected to implement. He even went so far as to question the initiation of the new feedback process.

Jerry not only questioned everything going on around him, he also saw alternate ways of understanding and interpreting things, and getting work done. His logic was not always instantly apparent. It seemed to many that he could not accept anything as fixed and decided. He slowed down meetings by offering alternative views on each subject discussed, always digging deeper before he agreed to move on.

And yet, the 380 people on his operating team loved him and delivered higher results than any of the similar operations in the New Bern plant or at competing facilities.

You can image what resulted when managers were given the opportunity to give Jerry feedback. The unrehearsed and unanimous consensus was that he should question less and give in more quickly to the majority view so that things could move forward. This was listed as an objective on his coming year performance improvement form, along with several other suggestions for change, including complaining less (he had never seen his engagements as complaints) and being less negative (he never understood them as negative).

Jerry put each of these items on his to-do list. Six months later, he was gone from the plant, and his group's stellar results exited with him.

I will revisit the story of Jerry's collision with feedback later, along with the shocking problem it created for the New Bern management team. I see the same downside to feedback over and over with other clients, and no real upside to compensate for it. Why do so many of us continue to rely on it?

Chapter 5

A Short History
of the Concept

The term *feedback* originated in the physical world of regulatory mechanisms. In particular, it was first used to describe closed (mechanical) systems in which dangerous or expensive flows of energy, fuels, or fluids are regulated in order to ensure safety, quality, and quantity. We are familiar with many of these systems in our everyday lives—for instance, gas pumps, which use feedback to prevent overflow when we are filling our cars. A mechanism in the nozzle's handle responds to a change in pressure and instantly closes the valve when a car's tank is full.

Another example is an electric pressure cooker, which shuts off when its valve cannot release pressure fast enough. And these days most of us have thermostats in our homes that regulate furnaces in order to sustain comfortable air temperatures. Feedback mechanisms are pervasive in the mechanical world and very useful. Their only purpose is to ensure that something rapidly stops flowing when necessary and then allows it to start flowing again.

Although feedback systems have existed since antiquity, it was not until the Industrial Revolution of the eighteenth and nineteenth centuries that the notion "to feed back" was recognized as a universal abstraction or concept. At that time, the phrase described only the action of "returning to an earlier position" via a mechanical process. In the early twentieth century, German

inventor and Nobel laureate physicist, Karl Braun, referred to the unantici-
pated coupling between components of an electronic circuit as "feed-back."
Within a decade of this use, audio feedback—the painful screech we hear
when a microphone is aimed toward an amplifier—brought the current term
into the dictionary. For most of the first half of the century, feedback was
defined as a specific type of *mechanical* action or effect.[3]

FIVE WORLDVIEWS

LIVING SYSTEMS PARADIGM

Knowing life as nested wholes, each alive, each uniquely expressing and evolving its potential; focus on working developmentally and acting nodally for systemic reciprocity

---

HUMAN POTENTIAL PARADIGM

A human-centered world concerned with human needs and expression; emphasis on emotional intelligence and experiential
transformation

BEHAVIORAL PARADIGM

Focus on physical existence; understanding of human behavior
based on analogies with plants and animals as metaphor; na-
ture-based recreation used as a method to relieve stress

MACHINE REDUCTIONIST PARADIGM

Focus on standardization, scaling up, replicability; activity
cascades top-to-bottom, reliance on trickle-down effects

ROYALTY AND ELITE PARADIGM

Elitism, a select few born or bred to lead others in war, government, and religion

By the 1950s, feedback became a concept of interest to theorists and acquired a more precise definition—"circularity of action"—albeit one still limited to physical mechanisms. Those who desired to make useful machines added to the meaning the notion of "deliberate effect" (via the connection of designed components).[4]

Feedback was not used in conjunction with psychological and human science theory until after 1940. The first known association was made at the Macy Conferences on Cybernetics from 1946 through 1953, part of a larger series of conferences sponsored by the Josiah Macy Jr. Foundation. The foundation held 160 international meetings in the years from 1941 through 1960, convening scientists and others from across diverse disciplines for the purpose of developing a unified path for all scientific endeavors.[5]

In the end, this effort leaned toward the physical sciences and swayed life scientists toward the machine worldview.

The Machine Worldview

Let's take a look now at the winds that blew science—and Western culture generally—away from whole-systems or living-systems ways of knowing, and toward a severely limited and mostly mistaken understanding of the human mind and behavior.

The machine worldview is one of a set of five historically related conceptions that provide most of us in Western countries with a shared interpretation of the way things work. Along with the behaviorist worldview, it is the primary foundation of modern corporate culture, and together they shape most business practices and the practices of all organizations that wish to operate with business-like efficiency.

Like worldviews generally, all five conceptions are based on societal values and beliefs, and have mainly to do with how we ought to conduct ourselves. We willingly conform to them because they help us make sense of life and our place in the world; they also provide us with a context for understanding and working with others, which makes our lives easier.

Worldviews vary by culture—for example, from atheist to Christian—and they define the possible range of discoveries and solutions within disciplines, such as sociology, history, musicology, and aesthetics. They also shape agreements between disciplines, framing them so that they align with one another and work together to describe how the world operates. Within disciplines or fields of endeavor, worldviews describe origins and provide coherence.

THE MACHINE REVOLUTION

The important technological changes of the Industrial Revolution that brought about the mass production of material goods also transformed business and work. A primary architect of the new work design was American mechanical engineer, Frederick Taylor, who sought to improve industrial efficiency and created what we now call "scientific management." He proposed that work could be done more efficiently, and at less expense, if the production process was broken into small pieces. Each piece would be assigned to a worker who could learn it easily and consistently repeat it over and over again.

Taylor was a fan of the economist, Adam Smith's, treatise on capitalism, which described this way of designing work systems as a narrowing or fine-tuning of focus. Like other intellectuals in this lineage, Smith imagined the human mind as a kind of clockwork and the universe as an infinitely complicated machine, set in motion by God and left to run on its own. Living systems and processes could be fully understood and mastered through the sciences of physics, chemistry, and mechanics. Historically, the worldview that grew out of this paradigm reduced workers to interchangeable cogs in machines connected in linear manufacturing processes. Work became rote, and because workers were believed to be easily replaceable, their safety and well-being were disregarded.

Based on the machine worldview, feedback entered management science via Cybernetics and Artificial Intelligence. As it evolved, it shaped business culture and systems throughout the second half of the twentieth century right up to today.

Cybernetics and Artificial Intelligence

Within the context of the machine worldview, two developments have contributed in a major way to current popular understanding of the human mind. The first is the work of physicist and science historian, Steve Joshua Heims, and the second was the theoretical models of psychologist, John Watson, who established the school of behaviorism based almost entirely on research with rats.

Heims interviewed attendees at the Macy Conferences on Cybernetics, and from their remembrances wrote up summaries of the conversations at the meetings, which had not been documented contemporaneously. These conversations explored the use of cybernetics, information theory, and computer theory as a basis for forming alliances among physical and life scientists.[6] They were structured along the lines of the framework used in artificial intelligence to understand large mechanical systems, leading to early adoption and integration of the metaphor of mind as machine into the definition of cybernetics.

The primary link between machine and human functioning was identified as feedback at a preliminary gathering in 1942 called, "The Cerebral Inhibition Meeting." According to the American Society for Cybernetics:

It was Arturo Rosenblueth's presentation of ideas he'd been developing with Norbert Wiener and Julian Bigelow that drew everyone's attention. Rosenblueth outlined a conceptual agenda based on similarities between behaviors of both machines and organisms that were interpretable as being "goal-directed." This goal-directedness (long spurned by hard science) was framed in terms of definitive and deterministic "teleological mechanisms." "Teleology" was transformed from philosophical mumbo-jumbo to concrete mechanism through the invocation of "circular causality" in a system, whereby new behaviors were influenced by "feedback" deriving from immediately preceding behaviors. This approach allowed one to address apparent [human] purposiveness with reference to the present and the immediate past, without having to invoke references to possible or future events [i.e. processing inherent in human intelligence, but invisible and therefore impossible to study and explain].[7]

From this it is clear that the bias toward the machine worldview way of understanding human behavior lay not only in the work of individual participants—including top minds from the worlds of mathematics, social science and sociology, medicine, psychology, anthropology, and linguistics, as well as many who worked on the Manhattan Project and the building of the world's first nuclear weapons. It also lay in the premises, questions, and topics around which their conversations were organized.[8] All of their thinking and discussion assumed that people are controlled by the outside forces that immediately precede their actions. In other words, we are not independent agents.

The second influence—behavioral theory and other psychological, medical, sociological, and philosophical contributions to the Macy conversations—also failed to consider any of the inner processing engaged that humans engage when making decisions, planning, and acting with intention. The dominant belief in the behaviorist paradigm was that this processing did not exist—or at least, it could not be observed objectively or scientifically researched. In the early twentieth century, when Watson established the school of behaviorist psychology, there were no instruments with which to "see" inside brains and study mental processes.

In an effort to make psychology rigorous along the lines of the physical science and thus to align it with the machine worldview, Watson rejected the traditions and insights of indigenous peoples, and the world's major religions and schools of philosophy. If the mind could not be studied objectively with mechanical devises, then he believed nothing could be known about it.

Heims evolved the information and understanding he took from his accounts of the meetings into a history of science. His focus was on cybernetics, and from his thinking, paradigms emerged that became central to the new fields of artificial intelligence and cognitive science. In particular, his work deeply influenced the direction of cognitive science, which focuses on human thinking and behavior.

Thus, it was Heims who further extended the mechanical concept of feedback as a metaphor for human behavior, coupled with behaviorist theory and the analogy of human motivation with the observed behaviors of rats. Over time, feedback became a dominant paradigm, pervading behavioral science and organizational practice. This transfer to human psychology was accomplished despite the fact that neither mechanical processes nor observations made from the study of rats are in any way adequate to describe human mental processing or behavior.

The adoption of cybernetics as a basis for conversations about human biological and neurological processes is indicative of the fragmented, linear, and extremely biased thinking in the very conception of the entirety of the Macy Conferences. Although the Macy Foundation intended for the meetings to be interdisciplinary and to give equal weight to life sciences, especially medicine, the conference did not include any living systems theorists.

This was especially significant given the prominence of the theory that the mind or consciousness could not be studied. The leaders of the Macy Foundation apparently accepted this, adopted most of the cyberneticists' language and thinking, and extended their metaphors into a way of pursuing knowledge, including technological research.[9]

CHAPTER 6

FEEDBACK AND HUMAN CAPACITY

As knowledge about cybernetic systems in computer applications grew (and eventually became information technology or IT), the process of providing feedback to peers, subordinates, and even superiors became popularized as the 360-degree performance appraisal. The creators of artificial intelligence systems had discovered the critical importance of feedback loops for correcting and adjusting mechanical system performance. It occurred to them that a similar mechanism—comprising of objective observation, appraisal, and communication—could provide corrections and adjustments to human behavior in business and other settings.

On the face of it, applying ideas about mechanical systems directly to human behavior seems questionable. Could people not use their common sense to discern that machines and human brains are differently constructed with different functions and capabilities? It turns out that, in fact, the very way living brains function worked against the likelihood of this insight.

The undeveloped human mind tends to think metaphorically in order to make sense of itself and what goes on around it. The desire to construct mental images of the way things work is part of our genetic makeup (see Ned Hermann's Whole Brain□ Thinking, for example[10]). But this nascent capacity must be developed before we can use it well. Imaging (seeing something in our mind as it actually works) is different from imagination (making up an explanation), which often seeks to transfer knowledge from what we think we understand already. We extrapolate inappropriately without examining the nature of what we may not understand.

For example, we think we can learn how to function well as humans by comparing ourselves to a forest, or beehive, or ant colony. Or, as Watson did, by studying the behavior of rats in mazes and transferring that narrative to the ways people work. This is an erroneous extrapolation of the worst kind because a rat in a maze in a laboratory, it goes without saying, is not even approximately a human living in the world. Information garnered from observing rats in highly artificial situations cannot approximate a true view of humans imbedded in nature and functioning naturally. The rat-to-human comparison is untrue to both species, transferring only the rat's thing-ness to the human, a purely physical and therefore false equivalency. Another example of this kind is imagining that a household cleaning product does its work in the same way that a leaf might be said to scrub air and water in a forest.

Feedback Undermines the Three Core Human Capacities

To develop the three core human capacities, a person must be self-directed. Inner processing is the only way to shift from external to internal locus of control, to broaden one's scope of considering, and to build personal agency. Only I can examine, interpret, understand, and move forward on what I experience. No one can do that for me. I must also be self-directed in my effort to acquire the mental skills needed for productive inner processing because fostering those skills is not part of our Western upbringing. In fact, it is rare today even in indigenous cultures around the world. Only when people come to see that they are giving away their control to others can they begin to break the cycle.

Feedback, by definition, is other-directed; we tend toward increased external locus of control and internal considering when we are constantly fed other people's interpretations of our ideas, emotional expression, and behavior.

Feedback also makes us wonder and worry about how others see and value us, which displaces our concern for others, and causes us to become more and more self-absorbed and self-centered. Our maturation processes reverse themselves, and we become like narcissistic children, emotionally stunted, and prone to dramatization and acting out.

The courage to examine our own shortfalls and successes depends on the practice of personal agency. Feedback, which is experienced as directives from others, effectively weakens personal agency, and fosters hierarchical social organization and a culture of authority. Most of us constantly received feedback in childhood. But children allowed to be independent in safe environments, to take risks and manage their own time, grow up with strong, self-directed agency and are far less affected by peer pressure or likely to need adult correction.[11]

It is also possible to shift children from the tendency for dependence on constant attention and feedback simply by trusting their capability. We can encourage and guide them with questions like, "How did you make this? How does it work? Why does it work this way? What do you think about that? Could it work better? How? What could you do to make that happen?" These are pretty much the same questions that adults with well-developed personal agency ask themselves from moment to moment as they work, raise their children, and participate in governance. The only difference is that they are so deeply ingrained in adults that we no longer hear them, only experience them in the shape and flow of our imaging, feeling, and thinking.

For increasingly full development, all three of the human capacities require us to be self-directed with significant reduction in our dependence on external influence, input, and management. Feedback, although it is not the only inappropriate controlling business practice, is the most invasive. It is the most likely to hinder our efforts to be self-governing and make beneficial contributions at all levels of our work.

CLOSED AND OPEN SYSTEMS:
HOW FEEDBACK ENTERED THE WORKPLACE

The metaphor of governance inherent in the general idea of feedback was suggestive of processes in the new participative business cultures. To many leaders, it seemed logical to assume that people rely on feedback loops similar to those in mechanical systems in order to govern their behavior. They assumed that human behavior in the moment, like machine behavior, was determined by immediately preceding interventions received as feedback. Thus, a misconception occurred in the transfer of the idea from the mechanical arena to the human world of business, as the result of insufficient understanding of cybernetic principles and inappropriate assumptions about differences and similarities in the natures of the two systems, machine and human being.

The most fundamental difference between a machine and a human being is that a machine is a closed system and a human is an open system. A closed system cannot function indefinitely without the addition of energy or a refill of fuel from an external source. An open system works through an energy *exchange* with its greater environment in a way that creates a symbiotic relationship. In order to work without running down, a machine is entirely dependent on an outside agent to supply it with fuel: a car needs to be filled with gasoline to move, a furnace requires a pipeline of oil or gas to burn, and a lamp must be plugged into an electrical socket to glow.

Human beings, on the other hand, work reciprocally with their environments and maintain relationships with them. People and their environments connect to one other and affect each other's survival through the interaction that takes place—as in a farmer-soil or customer-supplier exchange, or a marriage. They are interdependent and dynamically interrelated as open systems that fuel one other (or not) by implicit or explicit agreement.

In the application of the feedback metaphor to human systems, a misunderstanding arose when the machine's necessarily one-sided dependence on external controls was conflated with the human being's option to act independently of external considerations. In the resulting confusion, human behavior was reduced to the mechanical, and a popular notion arose that people need feedback from outside agents. The science of behaviorism added a final blow by asserting (without basis) that no internal process for self-regulation exists in humans that can be observed and experimented upon for confirmation. In the eyes of behaviorism, people simply could not be self-observing, self-understanding, and self-directed by drawing from guidance within themselves.

Delving a little more deeply into the function of a mechanical system can shed more light on this misunderstanding. In the closed system of a furnace, for example, a mechanism called the "governor" makes adaptation to changing external conditions possible. The governor is a second mechanical system that registers deviations from specified boundaries; that is, it senses and signals that heat production is too high compared to a preset temperature level. The governor uses this feedback to restore the operation of the larger system, the burner, to within the boundary, thereby returning it to conformity with preset standards.

However, complex open systems like people do not *need* to be externally informed or to import energy from an external governor in order to function. Humans do not have the same clear boundaries with their environments as machines. It is not always clear who controls what. Also, unlike mechanical governors, humans engage and interpret their environments with intellect and emotion, sense the states of other living systems, and observe their own processes as they simultaneously reflect and take action. Human intelligence is self-informing and self-adjusting, and consequently human actions can be self-governed.

In this way, people have the internal capacity to recognize behavior that has gone out of bounds. The value they place on this and the actions they require of themselves to change what they see is a matter of personal development, not imposed design. With the right resources, anyone can develop a highly nuanced, complex, realistic, and personalized understanding of the world and how it works, their relationship to it, and how they can make it better. For most of us, unfortunately, there is not much opportunity or much encouragement to develop our core capacities and the capabilities they foster, especially now after decades of applying the closed-systems theory to humans.

Fundamental flaws exist in the logic of introducing feedback into businesses (and families and schools) as a way to develop increasingly participative workers and more self-managing teams. The nature of human beings provides for a far more sophisticated and qualitatively different capacity for internal self-management than the mechanistic governance available to machines and other closed systems. Even in the case of the machine, the sensor and the governor are integrated. Perhaps all along it would have made more sense to attempt to understand machines in living systems terms than to understand living systems as clocks and other machines.

Part Three

Downsides To Feedback

Chapter 7

Flaws in the Theory of Objective Feedback

In addition to the differences between mechanical and human functioning, another challenge exists with applying feedback to our behavior. A machine does not have the ability to image itself and project its distinctive way of working or its own shortfalls onto another machine. The natures of machines, the boundaries between them, and their relationships with one another are fixed, unchangeable except for entropy and the gradual wearing out of their parts.

Humans, on the other hand, can develop the capacity to see their own shortfalls and to become self-observing and self-directed. Unfortunately, as we have seen, this developmental path is not currently well founded in most of our human systems. We also have not discovered ways to really see the truth of others. Equal to our potential for self-awareness, humans have not yet fully developed their capacity for empathy, objective assessment, and the kind of caring that leads to work on the full realization of human potential.

The latest research tells us that we are bad at understanding others because we have conditioned biases—and also because we tend to project our own shortfalls onto others. For example, we often tell people that they do not listen well when we are the ones who are bad at listening. We project onto them what we cannot afford to see in ourselves because we do not have the instruments required to change. This tendency to be blind to our own nature and project it onto others is well documented and widely accepted by psychologists, as is the fact that those on the receiving end of projections usually fail to notice them.

It goes without saying that feedback is not immune to projection, even when it is formalized as part of personnel assessments. Givers of feedback often project things onto other people with total confidence that are actually true about only themselves. Positive or negative, these projections are seldom apparent to either person or third-party witnesses. And in these formal processes—as a result of some cognitive biases—the recipients may accept false information and observations about themselves that do not fit their situations or behaviors. This natural defense against our own unconscious impulses or qualities (again, both positive and negative) denies them in ourselves and attributes them to others. That is truly deadly to the clarity and objectivity of feedback in performance appraisals, coaching, or any process in which one person is entrusted with making and sharing objective observations about another person.

The primary assumption is that an individual is less able to be objective about their own experience than someone else, which echoes the lessons of the machine and behavioral worldviews. For some reason, we assume that the observer is neutral and can see the truth while the person under observation is clouded by their own biases and interpretation.

It is true that people observing themselves have attachments to their way of viewing events, and the meanings and implications of those events. (And, of course, the same is true for the outside observer.) But these biases and attachments can be overcome, or reframed, with the development of a particular set of skills not usually seen these days in the West—and rare even in other times and places. Developing these skills in ourselves and others is one of the most urgent needs and greatest opportunities of our day. We will come back to them shortly but first let's question the idea that outside observers have no biases.

THE LIMITS OF OBJECTIVITY: COGNITIVE BIASES

You might assume that if multiple people provide the same input, the output will be accurate. But group-projection processes exist that work strongly against objectivity. In fact, several cognitive biases can sway people collectively toward false conclusions.

The human brain is powerful but subject to limitations, especially when those powers have not been fully developed. A cognitive bias is a type of error in thinking that occurs when people are processing and interpreting information in the world around them. Cognitive biases frequently result from the brain's attempt to simplify information processing, and they are often related to social conditioning. They also develop when we are not taught to control the quality of our thinking in diverse situations. Cognitive biases are rules of thumb that help us make sense of the world and reach decisions with relative speed, but like most mental shortcuts, they undercut our intellectual ability to be objective and thorough.

When we make judgments and decisions, we like to think that we are objective, logical, and capable of taking in and evaluating all of the available information. Unfortunately, the less self-aware we are, the more likely we are to be tripped up by biases, which lead us to make poor decisions and bad judgments. Most of the common biases that distort our thinking have been identified, and the ways that they distort our perspectives of other people's behaviors have been described by contemporary psychology.[12] All restrict high quality observation and objective interpretation of other people's behavior and intentions. Here are a few:

- Confirmation Bias: We tend to believe that we know people and things well enough to discern significant differences in their behaviors over time. In fact, we form and hold ideas early on and usually fail to notice or question changes, especially when what we think we know matches our strongly held views. This bias favors information that conforms to our existing beliefs and discounts evidence that does not conform.

- Availability Heuristic: In today's world, we move rapidly and need to make quick judgments. Because we are judged by others on our ability to be smart and act fast, we value our rapid-fire ideation and trust it. However, what we are actually valuing is not accuracy but looking smart by coming up with quick answers. This places greater value on speed and quantity than on quality. We give greater credence to information that comes to us quickly than to what occurs to us later, and we tend to overestimate the probability that what we observed in the moment will reoccur. We project our current ideas into the future, and this makes us even less likely to see significant changes.

- Halo Effect: All of us have heard the saying, "Do not judge a book by its cover" or "You'll never get another chance to make a first impression." Both can be true. We do tend to form an impression when we meet someone that changes very little over time. In fact, we tend to mistake an immediate, overall impression for a reliable assessment of a person. This impression then influences how we feel and think about his or her character going forward. This applies especially to physical attractiveness, which further influences how we rate other qualities.

- Self-Serving Bias: This is the tendency to blame external forces when bad things happen and to credit ourselves when good things happen. It is based on our lack of development of the three core capacities—locus of control, scope of considering, and source of agency. According to this bias, when I win a poker hand, it is due to my skill at reading the other players and knowing the odds. When I lose, it is because I was dealt a poor hand. This way of perceiving reality plays into our thinking when we are reviewers in feedback processes. We tend to gauge our own chances of being benefitted or harmed by the effects of our feedback rather than its usefulness to the recipient, and we can be unaware of or unwilling to manage this bias.

- Attentional Bias: This is the tendency to pay attention to some things while simultaneously ignoring others. When making a decision on what to notice about a person, we may pay attention to whether and how often they agree with us while also ignoring their ideas, especially when we are envious of them. We may even copy those ideas and take credit for them without noticing that we are doing so. We tend to downplay or ignore what is uncomfortable when we are interpreting observations and experience. This can profoundly bias our overall understanding of others' behaviors.

- Functional Fixedness: We often develop a tendency to believe that a familiar object can work only in the particular way we have seen it work in the past. If we do not have a hammer, we might never consider that a big wrench also can be used to drive a nail into a wall. We may think that we do not need certain skills because they are not directly called for in our fields, even though with some reflection we can see that they would benefit us in other ways. For example, writing may not be part of one's job but writing can improve one's thinking.

This bias can extend to an individual's functions within an organization. A supervisor may not realize that an assistant has the skills to assume a leadership role. Seeing people as fixed in their skills and character, especially if those assessments are dated, causes us to judge people based on old ideas versus seeing their potential. This limits our ability to support the growth of others with feedback.

- Anchoring Bias: Anchoring is the tendency to rely too heavily on the very first experience or information that comes one's way, rather than waiting to learn more before forming an opinion. When this bias is at work, we view the way we do something the first time, depending on the outcome, as either the best or worst way to do the same thing in the future. Having formed the opinion, we can fail to see that how someone else does the thing may be more effective than our way. Our minds are closed to further learning, which may rob our feedback of value.

- Misinformation Effect: Misinformation received after an event or an experience with a person can interfere with your original memory of the event or person. This could also be called the "gossip effect." It is easy to be swayed by second-hand information, and this can lead to the development of conformity in group thinking in preparation for a feedback cycle.

Psychological research identifies and describes dozens of other cognitive biases, but these eight, specifically, have the power to severely limit the objectivity of reviewers during feedback.

The Scourge of Race and Gender Bias

Two biases that cross all other known biases and are invisible to those of us who have not experienced them are race and gender. Groups tend to unconsciously collude around these biases, making it seem that there is consensus in feedback that incorporates them.

Because race and gender bias often are hidden even from persons adversely affected by them, they are more difficult to rout out than cognitive biases.

Whole cultures have developed them based on false assumptions, implicit social agreements, and self-centered cultural conditioning.

Abundant, reliable research now exists on the ways different races and genders experience one another, and how these internal frames of reference determine our mutual engagements. For example, the high incidence of murder and constant violent abuse by police of African Americans in many communities are the consequence of systemic racial bias. Undeserved suspicious attention paid to people of color who are not in any way behaving in ways that need to be monitored or managed is the result of these biases embedded in whole swathes of populations. Military institutions are characterized by bias toward women and the LGBTQ population. Racial, gender, and sexual biases began to shift in major ways in the twentieth century, and improvements are ongoing, but the basic cultural frameworks remain in place in the minds of older generations. There is no reason to believe organizations have succeeded in excluding the effects of these biases from their feedback programs. Bias marches through every feedback structure and process. Even the best training in how to give feedback fairly does not include developing mindfulness sufficient to observe one's own biases when evaluating other people's behavior and performance.

Because those people whose observing and thinking are most colored by cognitive, race, and gender biases have little capability to notice them, they are likely to go undetected in feedback processes. This makes it almost impossible to account for biases in any explicit way or understand them well enough to identify them when assessing the validity of the feedback. It is rarely effective for a person who has been misperceived due to another's bias to make a complaint. Although this is becoming less so over time, as individuals and societies develop more awareness of major biases, it is still a major limitation to the efficacy of feedback.

So much for the objective observer giving objective and therefore reliable feedback—or even for covering all the bases by having multiple people review a person. Groups of reviewers are far more likely to fall into group think than they are to get to a truth.

Even so, you might think that you can train people to manage their biases and design systems to avoid them. You can! And this is wonderful news. But to train or design processes so that those giving feedback can manage biases is doing it the hard way or, as we say, "going around your elbow to get to your ass." Why not instead focus on developing people to see the nature of their own and others' biases for themselves and skip the feedback from 'so-called" unbiased *others* altogether?

CHAPTER 8

FEEDBACK AND HUMAN
SELF-REGULATION

What happens when you manage people and businesses with feedback as if they were closed systems? It enhances the false premise that people cannot see into themselves and understand their own behavior—a false notion that has been drilled into them for most of their lives. And it causes a painful disconnect between how people experience themselves and what they hear from others.

Consider the case of a small firm in Silicon Valley, which touted itself as innovative and adopted 360-degree feedback.

UNEXPECTED DOWNSIDES: THE DIMINISHMENT OF SELF-REGULATION

Casandra, the company's HR manager, was an unusually aware person. She paid attention to how people responded to new programs introduced with her department's assistance. She formed internal focus groups and talked to people a lot about their experiences. Plus, she participated in all the programs as they were rolled out and experienced them as an insider.

Cassandra read about and did a lot of planning for 360-degree feedback work based on Franklin Covey's highly popular book, *The 7 Habits of Highly*

Successful People, with great ideas like building trust. What could go wrong? The company rolled out the program over two years to make sure they got it right.

One year in, several disturbing signs emerged, which Casandra admits she tried to ignore. Here is what she noticed:

1. People were becoming less connected to business outcomes and more concerned about themselves and how others saw them. This is self-centered internal considering, the opposite of system-actualizing external considering. Internal considering seemed to arise in people regardless of whether they were getting overall positive feedback or mostly negative feedback. Casandra had an idea about how to calibrate for this with better goals programs and decided not to worry about it.

2. Many employees' attention seemed to be increasingly focused on fitting in. Casandra had been with the business for seven years, from the time they were a start-up. In the beginning, each person saw themselves as responsible for the business and for bringing their unique gifts to the work. Casandra now noticed that people's desire to look like others—rather than express their uniqueness—was more and more prominent and becoming a competitive way of viewing performance. She told me that she thought this was a leadership problem and considered the possibility of adding a coaching program on how to bring out the best in each person by improving feedback.

3. These problems emerged at the same time as the introduction of competencies to help make feedback fair and balanced. Managers were taught fair-and-balanced as a core foundation for building trust into the 360-degree process. The idea was to focus everyone on the same measures of success and avoid singling out people, which could feel less like constructive feedback and more like personal criticism.

However, it quickly seemed clear to Casandra that competencies resulted in generic behavior. Individuality was shunned as focus shifted to the competencies and how well people were doing at developing them. Who was best at being fair and balanced; who was falling behind? Trust was to be ensured at any cost. Feedback was scary enough without feeling singled out.

Two years later, Casandra admitted that all of these downsides were evident within a short period of time, but she felt the unintended consequences of feedback would disappear, be ameliorated with other programs, or be worth it in the end based on improved performance. By the time it was obvious that the program was failing, the number of add-ons and corrections to the 360-degree feedback process was so large and so intricately interwoven—convoluted, really—that unraveling them seemed impossible. When I arrived as an educator to work with the company, it seemed like a sticky, tangled web, and it was hard to tell where to snip threads or undo knots. The question became whether to keep adding additional ameliorations and maintain the program or scrap it and start something else. The problem was that no one had come up with a better idea. The idea of self-directed behavior had not occurred to the company's leaders, and what they were doing instead was making everybody less and less self-regulating. Everyone in the program felt trapped.

In the way we do, people still tried to do their best on projects and their work. But they were not building the capability to regulate themselves, self-reflect, and understand how feedback might be useful if the process was redesigned based on realizing everyone's (and the business's) true potential. Turnover started to climb a bit, and the organization slowly became politicized. People were talking a lot in not very skillful ways about their own feedback and about the system. Trust eroded and so did individual creativity. This was the 180-degree opposite of what had been hoped for when the 360-degree program had been introduced.

SELF-REGULATION IS HUMAN NATURE

Part of Casandra's problem was that she and her company were misunderstanding human nature, including our driving desire to be self-regulating. Machines have no thoughts, and so of course they accept feedback without it diminishing them. Casandra was experiencing firsthand how the transfer of the machine metaphor to human systems sets in motion the disastrous introduction of beliefs and practices that are toxic to human potential and realization. In her case, it was a painful encounter with the foundational misconception that humans need to be controlled and directed with external feedback.

FIVE TYPES OF SYSTEM: MACHINE TO ECOSYSTEM

At this juncture, in order to understand why self-regulation is innate to humans, it may be helpful to consider that the term *system* has many different meanings and describes a variety of ways of working. Computers have become a default association with the word, regardless of the fact that they require human minds to create and direct them. There are five contexts or types to which the term is applied, ranging from mechanical to mental, and beyond mental to ecosystem. They all are valid for their place and use but they are not transferrable. These contexts from highest order to lowest, are:

FIVE TYPES OF SYSTEM

EVOLUTIONARY

DEVELOPMENTAL

ADAPTIVE

CYBERNETIC

MECHANICAL

MECHANICAL SYSTEMS are closed systems, with limited access to systems outside of their boundaries and a tightly circumscribed ability to exchange energy with them.[13] They are subject to wearing out and running down because of an inability to import or exchange energy in any integral or permanent way. A machine has no ability to import energy in order to organize and rebuild itself or replace deteriorating parts, and it is fully subject to entropy, the second law of thermodynamics.

Further, it is not possible for a closed system to go beyond its initial conditions, according to Karl Ludwig von Bertalanffy, an Austrian biologist known as the founder of general systems theory. The system's primary objective is to work to reduce entropy or increase *stabilization*, because this is paramount for its survival.[14] In industry, operators in a production system are acutely aware of this objective when it comes to their production line. They must keep products within certain tolerances and standards or they degrade to reduced or no value for the customer. This explains why mechanisms are built on assembly lines and maintained to ensure stable outcomes. An example is the electronic or mechanical testing equipment that manages chemical or physical components of base materials at each stage as they are transformed.

The energy in mechanical systems is what John G. Bennett, a British mathematician and scientist, referred to as vital, or life-giving, energy.[15] The material production system, itself, uses materials that are taken from the earth and transformed to give them higher value. Any aware person who has spent time in a production facility has experienced the line's life-giving quality (or the lack of it), the important role played by raw material, and the essential roles that people play in work with closed systems. Human energy is required to fuel closed mechanical systems, continuously and repeatedly, with life-giving materials and human energy, and with energy from the various supporting materials and mechanisms that ecosystems and humans also provide.

CYBERNETICS SYSTEMS thinking has become synonymous for many people with the term *systems thinking*, as we saw in an earlier chapter. The study of cybernetic systems is essentially the study of the theory of messages or information. Much recent development in the field is a phenomenon of the computer revolution, based on modeling, replicating, or simulating human activity, particularly brain activity. Mathematician and philosopher, Norbert Wiener, anthropologist, Gregory Bateson, and the core group at the Macy Conferences on Cybernetics were primary contributors to the development of this field.

Weiner noted that all information is subject to disorganization in transit, resulting from nature's tendency to degrade organization and destroy meaning.[16] The objective of cybernetic systems, he said, was to continue to function or operate in the environment as a result of or in spite of the interactions they have with their environments. The operational feature of a cybernetic system, therefore, is primarily a response or control based on feedback received from the environment. A person who seeks to establish an automatic heating system that does not rely on someone continually adjusting the temperature establishes the set point in a feedback system—in this example, a thermostat. This regulatory mechanism is the means used to achieve homeostasis and avoid system runaway (overheating).

In business settings, an analogy to the mechanical set point can be seen in the use of customer feedback or employee surveys to gauge the climate in their unit's workplace, especially when it is a routine and regular part of business activity. Here, homeostasis is sought to prevent loss of customers and ensure a steady state in employee morale.

COMPLEX ADAPTIVE systems are built to regulate and balance energy exchange in symbiotic relationships between entities and their environments. The work of von Bertalanffy and other biologists and systems scientists provides a clear picture of complex adaptive systems, often referred to as *open systems*.[17] A close link between cybernetics and complex adaptive systems thinking exists today because many of the systems concepts developed in the 1960s and 1970s drew on cybernetics to move toward open systems, particularly in their application to human systems.[18]

Complex adaptive systems and open systems exchange energy with their environments and can change and adapt in ways that go significantly beyond cybernetic systems. Complex adaptive systems are not, however, equivalent to living systems (a confusion that has arisen as the descriptor *living systems* has become popular in organizational development circles). In fact, the development of living systems theory over the last few decades has moved to encompass qualities and capabilities far beyond those normally ascribed to complex adaptive systems. This development has opened the door to the additional levels in the hierarchy, which suggests that we still have much to understand.

The objective of complex adaptive systems thinking is to create and maintain the effectiveness of a nonliving system, such as an agency or business, in relationships with other systems within a continuously dynamic and evolving environment. Because the system and its environment are exchanging energies, they affect one another whether they intend to or not. At the global industrial level, this can be seen in businesses working to build relationships with local governments and to adapt to regional and local preferences. Most energy is expended in sensitivity to changes in the relationship. The heterostatic mode is activated when the system detects challenges to laws or principles that it considers to be fundamental or inviolable to its capacity to maintain its integrity or its coherence as a being.

DEVELOPMENTAL SYSTEMS thinking turns the mind outward by bringing about an introduction of consciousness (seeing and self-managing our own way of thinking and acting with a purpose as a guide). This thinking enables a person to transform themself into something different—a self that is of service to the present and future benefit of other and greater systems. Another possible term for this level is *purposeful systems* thinking.

Complex adaptive systems thinking focuses organizations on their own vitality. When the viability of the greater system is at stake, it becomes clear that the development of the core human capacities is needed, as well as capabilities unique to particular individuals. Because our minds are trained within the context of mechanical metaphors and behaviorist thinking, which have established seemingly tried and true ways of processing phenomena, we are not very good at recognizing and understanding developmental systems. Further, this capability can really only be grown to proficiency within a developmental process. In the frameworks of Charles Krone, *developmental* means, precisely, uncovering the full potential and expression of the unique essence of any entity or system, including necessarily the greater systems within which it is embedded.[19] Development can occur in a home, class-room, laboratory, factory, government office, or global planning meeting—anywhere that living beings engage with one another.

Scientists and the world's great spiritual traditions alike have published work on developmental thinking.[20] It makes sense: Development requires spiritual-izing systems or bringing in a new spirit. In business systems, developmental thinking is the reconceptualization of the business through an exploration of its core value, core process, and core purpose, and ways to manifest them uniquely. A business's people can only discover these interactively, by looking outward, beyond themselves and the business, itself, to the larger systems they collectively serve.

A developmental approach is based on a paradigm that sees every living entity (e.g. person, organization, community, ecosystem, nation) as having a unique essence or being that is searching for channels and means of expres-sion. This way of seeing the whole can easily become lost if there is a shift back to the internal focus on competitive ventures.

Thinking developmentally, an organization would ask itself what is at its core based on several points of reference. It would value processes that reveal the essences of individuals and find places for them to contribute to its singular direction, which is one that offers greater value to stakeholders from the beginning to the end of its value-adding process. In the business, managers would come to see people as unlimited in terms of increasing essence expression in their service to greater purposes. Businesses and other organizations rarely accomplish this shift to developmental thinking as a whole because it takes designing and utilizing processes to develop people beyond their current mindsets.

Because currently there is a big demand in business for ways of developing people, most companies—even when facing the gut-wrenching experience of losing their existence—operate as cybernetic or, at best, complex adaptive systems, reacting or adapting as needed. But if a business or other organization takes on true development, it can find its essence and unique direction, and learn to think developmentally about all of its work, focusing on improving everything and every person to pursue that direction.

If we are to free ourselves of the machine and rat metaphors, we will need to return to ways of developing the three core human capacities, nascent in all of us. In this way, we have the potential to create opportunities for people to fully mature and express themselves—in other words, to live up to their human potential.

EVOLUTIONARY SYSTEMS thinking compels organizations to let go of certainty and, in some arenas, to drive toward defined outcomes or purposes. Sometimes it becomes apparent that the field of study or discipline in which creative processes take place must be seeded with a distinct way of thinking and being in order to bring something truly renewing into existence. The purposes supported by developmental systems thinking are ephemeral moments in evolutionary paths. What leadership is seeking is organizations that focus on increasing generative potential by increasing creativity and raising it to higher orders.

When you are working to increase the generative capacity of a field, you know that you can no longer predict the trajectory of players in the field. Yet what you care about most is this search for a set of generative approaches. This nature of energy is focused on customers, communities, nations, and other stakeholders, wishing for each to raise its capacity to the level of generation. An organization working from evolutionary systems thinking sees its primary purpose as regenerating the field and seeking to harmonize with the direction in which it seems to be unfolding. It is working with what does not yet exist, and thus building intelligence at different levels of systems thinking becomes critical.

An organization that works *regeneratively* seeks to source new potential to be generative for the process (the way of working), the producer (worker), and the product (the result of the work). This level might also be called, as I have called it before, *regenerative systems thinking* because evolution is the primary purpose and work of regeneration.

An example of regeneration might be an Amish farm, which provides a spiritualized context within which family and workers become creative in regard to the quantity and quality of farm output. They simultaneously improve soil health and biological diversity by improving the overall means of growing and farming. Whereas a developmental organization seeks to make improvements based on its essential nature and purpose; the evolutionary system understands that it can only regenerate itself by fostering generative players in the field who are constantly resourcing themselves from a deeper well of intelligence. In a business setting, this means looking at the entire value chain within the context of its industry and beyond to the systems in which the industry is nested and the even larger systems that these serve.

In the greater Amish community, evolutionary thinking might lead the regenerative farm to advance from working exclusively in local agriculture to working on nutrition as a system of its own. This in turn would generate a sense of stewardship for the entire value chain, from seed development to the nutrient quality of produce and its effect on health. An evolutionary process gives a new context to all levels of systems thinking—building a more comprehensive and ecological consciousness of all systems. The farm would return to improving its development process, its complex adaptive reciprocal processes, and its cybernetic systems. It would also build a closed system to safely recycle what once was considered waste into a useful, beneficial product.

What are the work practices appropriate for self-regulating human beings? How do organizations transition to them, and what are the benefits to be gained from doing so?

The first step is to challenge the premises from which most organizations currently operate and replace them with more useful ones, based on insights into the nature of the fully developed human brain and its potential to create beneficial effects in the world through clear-eyed perception and self-regulation. It is important to examine developmental premises consistent with human nature, comparing them with the false assumptions in place in most organizations. Because these are insidious and often camouflaged, it is necessary to make them explicit in order to discern how they are always counterproductive and often extremely harmful.

Part Four

Premises For Designing Developmental Work Systems

Chapter 9

Premise 1: Self-Governing Behavior is Energy Effective

The foundational element in effective work systems is self-correcting, self-managing, self-accountable, and self-governing behavior. Energy spent on monitoring and attempting to alter the behavior of team members or others from the outside is energy wasted—energy that could be better expended on improving the business and the capability of its people. The critical element in improving or evolving work systems is to increase the self-governing capability of everyone involved.

Self-regulating behavior is not only more effective, it is also entirely achievable when time is devoted to developing people's capacity for it and creating work systems that support it.

In most organizations, the current premise is that humans cannot be self-managing and must be managed from an external source. This arose, as we saw earlier, from the behaviorist worldview. Watson was wrong but his theories still control businesses and workers.

In Western cultures, we have systematically worked in ways that erode self-accountability in our families and organizations. First our parents, then our teachers, and finally our employers and supervisors tell us *what* to do, how well we *perform*, whether we meet a certain *grade* or *rank*, and to what degree our behavior is *correct*. In other words, they give us feedback. This is so deeply embedded in our way of operating that it is difficult to see its pervasiveness and how it works against creating self-accountable human beings.

Human energy is required to fuel closed mechanical systems, continuously and repeatedly, with life-giving materials and human energy, and with energy from the various supporting materials and mechanisms that ecosystems and humans also provide.

Even in cybernetics systems theory, mechanical and electrical systems operate effectively only through the regulatory control of built-in governors that sense and correct deviations from desirable norms. These nonliving governors use information to identify differences or changes that exist throughout the system, which indicates to them whether the system is operating optimally. This allows the system, in an *internally* managed, "self-correcting" manner, to work to regain an ideal or optimum state based on defined parameters. (Thus, the metaphor drawn from cybernetic theory—because it posits external rather than internal governors—is inaccurate even from the start.)

The assumption in most of our modern organizational settings that people cannot be self-governing or self-auditing is based mainly on the belief that they cannot be objective about themselves. Humans, even with a more complex brain, higher level of mental functioning, and ability to make reasoned choices, are assumed to be less able than machinery to be self-regulating. Unfortunately, this often proves to be the case for individuals but it is not innately characteristic of the species. If the ability to self-manage is not developed in us from childhood, our capacity to be self-reflecting (self-observing and self-remembering) steadily diminishes. This is particularly true when our primary source of reflection as we grow up comes from others and focuses on elements that pull us away from what feels intrinsically self-integrating.

An example drawn from a familiar experience can shed some light. Occasionally, when someone I respect urges me to take a particular course of action, I find myself silently objecting. When I do not listen to myself and go my own way, I lose my sense of integrity, of being my own person. This occurs in my life less and less often but when it does and I become aware of it, I am vividly reminded of the inner harmony that is fundamental to every person's course of development. People have a strong desire to feel this alignment between our values and our behaviors, even when we have to learn the hard way, by making painful mistakes. To act otherwise, especially to repeatedly follow the good advice of others without self-reflection, is to deny our own inner sense of reality and, in the most extreme cases, to become mentally ill.

When viewed through a developmental lens, it is possible to understand how a person, *any person*, can use a process of self-reflection to create self-regulating behavior. Reflecting on our thinking and the emotions behind particular behaviors provides us with *internally developed* insight and advice. It alerts us to the degree of adherence we are maintaining in our attempts to behave well according to standards we set for ourselves or to achieve particular aims.

With internal reflection, a person can tell what is uniquely optimizing and integrating for them. We forget sometimes that what we think requires changing in another person may not be the critical change needed from *their* perspective and that what works for one person does not necessarily work for another. This is a core life exercise in the development of self-accountability—discovering what works for us, what demands higher inner discipline, and what benefits from flexibility in our dealings with others and ourselves.

FEEDBACK VERSUS SELF-ACCOUNTABILITY AT DuPont

In DuPont's corporate engineering group, for example, the introduction of feedback as part of performance reviews was easily accepted. They had seen testimonials compiled by the consulting company hired to guide the process, and it all felt natural and appropriate to engineers who design systems based on feedback mechanisms.

Ed Klinge was the group's appointed organizational sponsor, chartered with bringing them into the twenty-first century with new technologies for performance management. Feedback would be introduced into an updated version of the current managerial performance reviews, which required the creation of a new process including new documentation and training. It was Klinge's full-time role and took him about 60 hours a week to educate himself and others about the process in the year leading up to full implementation. Still, it felt meaningful because he wanted to support a function and a company in which he deeply believed.

Training sessions were the most fun. Klinge taught people how motivation worked, how listening was critical, and that fairness was paramount. He was learning as much as he had in engineering school and told me the story of a young manager who asked him a stop-in-your-tracks question. Klinge was introducing skills for sharing hard feedback in cases of poor behavior. As the group practiced in pairs, the manager walked over to him and asked, "What if I'm misinterpreting the situation? I see people do that to me and others all the time. Are you going to teach us a way to assess whether we are right?"

Klinge admitted that this was not in the lesson and said they would learn by doing it over time. The manager's last comment as he went back to practice was that he hoped he wouldn't do too much damage while he figured it out.

A very experienced manager raised another concern. He wondered where they were going to get the time to do all of this on top of their regular jobs. Klinge's exchanges with this manager continued for several rounds while they continued training. In the end, the manager asked Klinge if the engineers could just do a better job of hiring the right people instead of trying to "feedback them into excellent performance."

Indeed, when Klinge performed an evaluation of the new review process a year later, the biggest surprise was how much time managers were spending on it. It had increased the average manager's workload by about 7 percent, and levels of anxiety remained high. When managers were asked what they thought about the process and its effectiveness, their responses were surprising.

Over the next few years, Klinge tried to find ways to improve feedback. *There must be a way to get it right*, he thought, and it took a full decade before he threw up his hands (metaphorically) and started looking for a better plan. The engineering group stopped all structured feedback processes and gave managers back their time, with no loss in productivity or performance. Then they instituted in feedback's place a process for building the ability to be self-managing in all of their people, and they revised their business philosophy to one based on self-accountability. This added a bit of new work but it was directed to running the business, not managing people's performance. In a short time, it paid for itself with a 35 percent improvement in financial effectiveness, measured as a return on investment from their group. This was far and away a much better use of Klinge and his team's time and creativity.

Chapter 10

Premise 2: Self-Reflective Capability Is Necessary for Self-Governance

The ability to be self-correcting or self-governing depends on the capability to be self-reflecting: 1) to see one's own processes as they play out, 2) to interpret them in terms of what is needed to return to homeostasis (balance and harmony internally and with one's environment), and 3) to create heterostasis (evolution and change of strata or class).

Returning to the cybernetics theory, we find that an internal mechanical governor seeks the relevant information for optimizing the *whole* of the system and interprets it to determine what is needed. It turns out that human beings have a similar drive to maintain wholeness and not be diverted into suboptimization.

Forcing information into a human or machine system, overriding its autonomy, will cause either *oscillation* (wavering or vacillating without any ability to choose or proceed independently) or *runaway* (overcompensation for an isolated piece of information). Oscillation and runaway, when repeated over time, produce increasing distortion and deterioration of the system's ability to rebalance or optimize. Both result from seeking to *maximize* the variables on which attention is focused over and above *optimizing* the overall system, which is the action sought by mechanical governors and human self-reflection.

A good understanding of this comes from the simple example of inner harmony from the previous chapter. We so consistently want to preserve our inner harmony that sometimes *the more* someone tells us to stop doing something, *the more* we resist stopping, in spite of the fact that it may hurt us. Sometimes their admonishments even escalate our behavior. One research study found that primary schoolchildren at a certain age could no longer correctly interpret whether they were following simple instructions. Instead, they defended their responses despite being shown photos of their mistakes. However, after only a few weeks of prompting to reflect on the accuracy of their responses to the same instruction, and without any external input, they became increasingly accurate at judging their own success. Although the capability to reflect on and correct our own behavior has been systematically eroded in our culture, it can be regained with practice and often in a short time.

In a human system, runaway—which results from focusing on a portion of the whole, rather than its entirety, or when ignored elements get out of control—cannot be maintained for extended periods of time without the system losing its ability to return to self-governance and self-correction. You will recognize this if you have raised a teenager.

To restore the system from runaway to self-correcting, it is important to reintroduce self-reflection. This must be done in such a way that the reflection can be used to *reoptimize* the whole; otherwise, the system's ability to learn and adapt will be eroded. For example, an autoimmune system challenged by chemotherapy may lose its natural ability to adapt and to determine which antibodies or types of blood cells to release and which to destroy.

In businesses, a comparable loss of adaptability results when teams take on a narrow task, such as attempting to regain control of costs following a period of intense focus on quality. The tendency is to attempt to shift the focus of the operating teams as fast as one can to each new runaway area with the hope of regaining control over the whole system. The result of this approach is that the organization becomes increasingly incapable of regaining its balance and integrity. Such businesses shift from cost to quality, and then when cost gets out of control, back to cost or safety, and from there back to quality or on to the next runaway. This method of correcting the imbalance manifests itself as unrelated, segmented goal setting in each of the recently out of control arenas.

The tendency toward runaway is similar in the case of a person who continually receives feedback from external sources. Focus is drawn immediately and intensely to the arena of highest attention from external observers. Whether the feedback is negative or positive, the response is the same. Focus is placed on changing what has been critiqued or mentally replaying the compliment or criticism over and over again. Either way, the person has lost touch with the inner integrity that is needed to ensure their evolution and development as a whole.

DuPont's New Plan

Once Klinge realized that DuPont needed a new path forward, he created a strategy group to explore the practices of other companies. The team created a set of criteria for companies on their list that, like DuPont, included "publicly held" and "good financial return." They wanted to test any new approach for at least five years, and they wanted the organization as a whole to feel good about the results.

The companies that showed up on their list included Procter & Gamble in Lima, Ohio, American Honda Motor Co, Inc., and a few others. Their first site visit to Procter & Gamble was "a real eye-opener," according to Chad Holliday, then head of the DuPont strategy group. P&G Lima had placed self-directed organizational members at the foundation of everything they did. They designed their own way of working from the ground up, not borrowing from any of the new programs emerging at the time, including feedback.[21]

Based on their new strategy, P&G Lima called themselves a "consciousness-based and will-driven" organization. They were building into their people the capacity to see and manage themselves through conscious awareness of their own actions and the effects they had on others. As a result, people were self-initiating and self-managing in a compelling strategic direction. The business was beating their competition on every scorecard, from financial return to shelf space and market-basket return for the distributor. The DuPont folks were impressed and also a bit awed.

What especially astounded them were P&G's methods. After nearly a decade of feedback programs, sometimes coupled with competencies, P&G companies had shifted and were relying primarily on an embedded, ritualized development process to grow their people's critical thinking skills and personal mastery. They were using organizational frameworks for advancing projects and creating changes to improve marketplace presence and their customers' lives, and they were operating with mostly independent management. They had tracking but no competencies. Instead, each employee evaluated their self-initiated work in terms of market outcomes and financial effectiveness. Klinge described the people at the P&G companies as filled with so much motivation to do great and meaningful work that watching them felt like "going to church." He meant that it was a greatly moving experience with lots of hallelujahs in praise of P&G's great changes.

Three of the five companies DuPont visited used the same methodology, what they called "a developmental approach to change and growth." They took conscious steps to give people more creation space. In fact, a condition of employment was the delivery of a significant, financially effective endeavor. Supervisors shifted from managing people to what they called "resource roles," serving individuals and teams who grew their business revenues by more than 35 percent annually.

At these companies, employee retention and competence were not a problem; everyone was maturing to the level of top talent. The return on people development was double to triple that of the return on the former management process. It was far more advantageous to grow people and give them freedom to lead than it had been to manage them with feedback that had no direct ties to market outcomes.

DuPont saw that the developmental organization plan was the one to pursue. Its foundation was to build deep capacity for self-reflection, self-initiation, and self-correction across the entire organization.

CHAPTER 11

PREMISE 3: THE BASIS OF SELF-REFLECTION AND SELF-GOVERNANCE IS A DEVELOPMENTAL PLAN

To work as a self-correcting system, individually or as part of a team, a person must operate from a developmental plan that contains three lines of work, stemming from a hierarchy of values and influences. This means working on expressing one's own uniqueness (first line) and learning about oneself and the joys and problems of working with others (second line), while all the time searching for opportunities to make a contribution to something greater than oneself (third line).

The only way a person can maintain their inner balance and optimize their ability to be self-governing is by creating and utilizing their own developmentally holistic plan and then continually self-reflecting to stay with the plan.

Cybernetics theory tells us isolating what is perceived to be an unintegrated part in a system to stay within predefined parameters will inevitably lead to runaway. In people, this occurs most frequently due to well-intentioned feedback from external perspectives. Feedback is useful information to a system only when it can successfully prevent oscillation or runaway. For people at work, any feedback is only even marginally useful in the context of what I call "third-line work." That is, any assessment is useful only if it serves efforts that are adding value to or benefitting processes and people that a greater whole system contributes to and depends on for reciprocal benefits. For example, when a doctor makes an honest and thorough assessment of her medical practice, she does so not just in reference to the healthcare system in which she works, she also considers its effects on her patients. She then factors in the effects these smaller systems (her clients) wish to have on the larger systems to which they make contributions and from which they receive benefits. These larger systems include their families, schools, workplaces, churches, and communities.

This perspective requires considering the whole of things. In the business world, the value-adding or third-line context comes from the customers and consumers of goods and services produced, as well as from those who hold a stake in a company's endeavors. In the context of third-line work, an individual determines which product or service increases the effectiveness of the customer; he or she then sets an appropriate plan to provide it. Enabling others to move beyond where they are always requires us to raise our own level of capability. In the context of all three lines of work, a person is able to *discern* feedback in the form of information received from external sources, and to interpret and make use of it through self-reflection and by further contextualizing it in their own developmental plan. This process requires discovery, leads to further self-reflection, and strengthens and improves the ability to be self-reflective.

The developmental plan is based on aims for customers or consumers that require us to develop beyond our present abilities and state of being. We take on these aims because we see things that need doing that we are uniquely able to accomplish. Based on aims for customers, aims also are set for the organization or business we propose to support or for the team to which we belong. In turn, we set personal aims required of us in order to achieve the other aims we have set—and thus all three lines of work are engaged. These aims are not the same as traditional goals and objectives; they are developmental paths that require us to *become* something different rather than just *do* something different.

What Is *Not* Developmental?

There are several "categorizing feedback" methods in vogue that are offered as training and development but are decidedly not developmental in their nature. The Myers-Briggs analysis is one example. These models tend mainly to be presented as static and categorical, inviting a better understanding of who we are but offering little or no opportunity to see the person we might become. They are standardized tests, primarily focused on the personality and functional aspects of an individual without a sufficient invitation to explore the uniqueness we have as whole human beings. In this kind of process, a person comes to see the self as static (what I am) rather than evolving (what I am becoming or could become) and as common (definable by external standards) rather than unique.

When these assessment models are used in organizations, they contribute to a field of external judgments whereby we see people as types within only a few categories. Their lives are reduced to boxes or ranks. Such static models are the Lorelei of developmental processes. Just as the legendary beautiful Lorelei lured sailors onto the rocks with enchanting songs, these methods captivate managers with promises they cannot keep.

Developmental Plans

Many organizational processes are called development plans but most really are only plans for training, created in response to a core competency or feedback assessment. They are not remotely developmental according to my use of the word. The following additional premises lay the groundwork for a truly developmental plan and can be used to assess the examples and stories that follow in the next section. It should be noted that individuals, teams and other groups, and whole organizations can create and pursue a developmental plan. I primarily refer to individuals here, but most of the information can be extrapolated to groups and organizations.

A) A developmental plan is founded on the idea of expressing potential rather than solving behavioral problems or performance shortfalls, or conforming to other people's standards.

B) The plan starts from a person's essence, not from behaviors or personality characteristics. Essence can be discovered or evoked in many ways, a few of which are hinted at in upcoming stories.

C) The person or group making the plan, and those resourcing them, assume that intrinsic motivation is the source of growth and development. They avoid generic, homogenized ideas offered from external sources or from people not engaged in this particular developmental process.

D) A development plan is effective when it includes taking on a challenge beyond the individual or group's current capabilities. It becomes even more effective when it is in service of a greater whole for the benefit of others (people, communities, ecosystems) who are valued and respected. This extension requires that the plan seek to have impact beyond one's set of friends, family or acquaintances, coworkers or cocreators, all of whom constitute what we call *second-line community*.

E) The structure but not its content can be shared across the organization or with the second-line community. In other words, a plan's outline can serve as a blank slate or starting place, unique within an agreed-upon framework with shared areas to consider. But the actual content of any individual's plan is unique to them and cannot be shared with or applied to any other person.

F) The boundaries of a developmental plan are provided by an organizational strategy—a compelling, meaningful promise beyond the organization's current capability to deliver unless individuals and work units engage in growth and collective effort. Such a plan cannot be tied to goals or other similar, recurring strategies that serve organization stakeholders.

G) The personal agency of the individual to whom the plan belongs is the primary guide and driver of the plan and its accomplishment.

H) The plan is evaluated and audited by the person who develops, pursues, and achieves its aims and by others invited by this person to share reflections within an agreed-upon framework.

I) Those who are invited to share reflections claim them as entirely their own observations and thinking (as in any active listening process). They do not belong to the person to whom they are offered. Reflections are examined by both parties using a shared framework to assess their relevance and usefulness.

CHAPTER 12

PREMISE 4: SELF-OBSERVATION AND RESOURCING DEVELOP THE CAPABILITY FOR SELF-REFLECTION

Self-observation and resourcing are two capabilities that are not usually well developed in modern cultures. Feedback has been introduced to fill the void that their absence creates with devastating consequences. Feedback prevents people and organizations from becoming aware of their inner processes and the effects of their work in the world. Both self-observation and resourcing are essential for building the capacity to create and work with plans based on developmental premises.

SELF-OBSERVATION

Self-observation is the ability to isolate aspects of yourself from your day-to-day life, standing apart to see the sources of your behavior and thinking, and to note your effects on others. Observing yourself, you are in a divided state; you are both the observer and the observed. This capability, though it is sometimes taught as mindfulness or meditation practice, is rarely developed in schools or businesses.

Self-observation allows a person to change or correct their own thinking, behavior, and effects on the outside world in the moments they occur. This capability, which grows only through ongoing practice over extended lengths of time, is boosted when a person engages with a community of people working together on developing it—especially when this community shares a dedication to second- and/or third-line work. To provide the basis for real change in the world, self-observation must be built into entire organizations as part of their developmental infrastructures.

RESOURCING

Acting as a resource to others on developmental paths contrasts sharply with some other leadership or guidance roles such as coaching, mentoring, training, facilitating, and giving feedback, which often inhibit or completely shut down the practice of self-observation. The term resource can be understood by breaking it into its parts: *Re-source*, to *return* someone to themself as the *source* of wisdom and knowing. This necessarily banishes the assumption that thinking, knowing, and wisdom have any place whatsoever outside individual self-observing minds.

In regenerative work, resourcing is conducted by Socratic questioning and the use of living systems frameworks. Together, these enable resources (those who provide resourcing) to pose questions without relying on a private agenda or judgment, and to work with the person they are resourcing in a more complete way. This naturally fosters self-observation on the part of both the resource and the person being resourced, and it eliminates suspicions that either is pursuing a hidden agenda or thinking off topic. The roles of resource and resourced are far and away preferable to supervisor and supervisee, or feedback presenter and feedback recipient because they foster development of the core human capacities in both parties, among other beneficial effects,

Resourcing development is unique in that it is based on the execution of a plan that the resourcing recipient created based on the distinctive self (the essence) they seek to manifest. Observations and assessments from others are accepted based solely on a prearranged contract. This contract contains the principles on which resourcing will be based, and it defines the arenas within which resourcing is invited. It requires that resourcing be conducted in the form of questions that foster self-reflection.

This kind of contract aids the development of self-governance and agency toward the developmental plan aims and enables individuals to evolve their essence and the contributions they seek to make to the organization's stakeholders (distinguished from those they make to the organization, itself). Holistic, optimizing assessment can come only from within oneself and from one's own reflections. Feedback from others, regardless of how skillful it is, always tends to be maximizing in nature, which invites runaway.

In business settings, the only effective feedback from an outside person is feedback that relates to the status of a project led by the feedback recipient. It may be a rise in margins or revenue, an expansion or extension of offerings, or sometimes communications (good or bad) from a distributor or consumer. These are targeted outcomes written into the developmental plan that have been deeply considered by a team selected to support the endeavor and resource the person leading it. The means of measuring have been specified and validated with the plan's creator, the project leader, and often in alignment with their stakeholders' objectives. Those conditions make it fairly easy to track outcomes and successes, and eliminate any need for the use of generic standards or competencies that do not invite people to be themselves or to innovate outside the box.

DEVELOPMENT AT DUPONT

In the lead-up to DuPont's change initiative, Klinge's first question to his hosts during visits to other companies was, "Why does your approach work so well? Why is it far outstripping all the other new practices?" Most hosts replied that there was no way to make comparisons because they were avoiding "programs of the day" that they knew from experience were toxic. They assessed the chosen practices based on their ability to achieve the three core human capacities and had sent consultants and academics out the door before they got far into the conversation. They knew that fostering the core human capacities would steer their businesses toward steady growth.

My own research—comparing cybernetics with human psychology based on living systems—provides a bit more insight into why the developmental approach works far better to drive change and course correction than the people management approach based on external inputs. We saw how feedback drives runaway thinking: Replaying others' observations and assessments, obsessing about whether they are true, comparing them endlessly with one's own opinions, and building arguments for or against them in our heads that we may or may not share with others. Whenever feedback is offered, it takes some time for all that mental recycling to run its course and for people to get back to their real jobs. It is obvious that this results in loss of motivation and direction, which further results in lost time, lost money, and lost creativity for the organization.

An unexpected and much worse outcome exists as well. Runaway thinking and speculation post-feedback invariably leads to decreases in individuals' capacity for self-reflection and a subsequent loss of self-governing capability. This may seem like a big jump, from a bit of destabilization caused by receiving feedback to serious loss of self-control. However, my research and reports from many companies that adopted feedback processes show that constant inner dissonance and mental defensiveness make people question themselves about what is true and, moreover, what really matters. Sometimes people end up working on things with which they do not agree, and often on activities that seem minor or a distraction from the real work. This phenomenon cannot help but erode whole organizations.

When people work from plans they created with built-in designs for specific contributions and development, they can extract and interpret the information, and convert it into optimizing self-observation and self-reflection. This kind of plan provides a whole context within which information received indirectly or from markets can be assessed and used for further self-development and contributions to stakeholders. Without this context, the interpretation of information always gravitates towards egocentrism or reactionism (at least for a time), which again makes optimizing responses difficult. No part of a living system truly can manage its own behavior independent of external engagements with other systems to ensure the vitality and viability of the whole. Real development or regeneration requires a community working together to build the core human capacities.

THE SOCRATIC METHOD

What about resourcing? I described earlier the use of Socratic questioning, which leaves learning and the strengthening of agency to the person guiding their own development. Socratic questioning is far more than the popular image of a foolish old man offering questions as a trail of bread crumbs to the right answer. Resources have no answers. They seek to make discoveries along with the people they are questioning. They stay with the inquiry, and even when they think they see something the other person is missing, they continue to ask questions, encouraging ever deeper reflection.

The Socratic method relies on five guidelines, which work together as a system to bring about this deeper reflection. It is a lost art and its practice is frowned upon in most US institutions; it does not work well for teachers who aim only to elicit stock answers. Its purpose is to ask questions that require intense reflection about a person's own experience and the effects their actions have had on themself and others. Students taught this way learn to think about hard questions, and find new ways to see and make sense of life and the world around them. They are able to observe their own minds, and they develop the ability to reframe what appeared to be difficult situations into opportunities for innovation. That was Socrates' intention—not to *teach* his wisdom but to ask questions that would *guide* students to wisdom by engaging them in structured reflection.

A way of learning that does not lead to immediate insights is difficult for some people to accept. Their concern is that not getting the answer quickly implies they are ignorant or slow learners. When children ask questions that require reflection, adults often are annoyed. Western science focuses on assessing the quality and validity of answers. Game shows and educational processes, too, reward memorizing and learning to produce rote answers.

We have virtually no way of learning to develop questions that challenge us to reflect or for assessing the quality of our questions. Training in question development, posing questions, or identifying pointless questions would better serve businesses and teams than the current focus on communicating predefined ideas to others. Questions are a source of newness and regeneration, and yet we spend 99 percent of our lives acquiring answers and learning how to get more answers. Posing open-ended questions creates a very different learning and work environment than asking questions with predefined answers, which casts parents and teachers in the role of expert rather than nurturer or cocreator. Feedback is teaching to the test; it holds everyone up to a single light, excluding creative differences and diminishing the will to think freely or even at all. True intelligence is measured by the quality of a person's questions, not by the number of correct answers.

The Value of Great Questions

A profound test of the value of questions in human development can be seen in a program developed at the University of Arizona for helping educators deal with slow learners. The program worked on fostering higher order thinking skills (HOTS) and used the Socratic method as the foundation for learning. Teachers asked questions instead of offering answers. The core belief was that children's cognitive development was paramount versus their ability to absorb facts.

The results posted by schools using the HOTS approach were remarkable, particularly in view of the fact that most of the students entering the program were considered to be remedial or at-risk. Ten percent were reclassified as gifted at the end of the first year, and slightly more than one-third made and retained a position on their schools' honor rolls. Of four students ranked as the top academic learners in one school, two were HOTS participants who rose from the bottom of their class.

In a single year, participating students gained an average of 15 percent on standardized reading and math test scores; they also scored 67 percent above the national average in reading and 123 percent above the national average in math. Significant improvement was noted in every student's self-concept. All reported feeling increasingly confident of success at levels well beyond those that they originally felt were possible. Also, at the end of the year, in one school students in the program no longer posed any discipline problems at all.

If you transfer this to a business setting, you can quickly see the power of working with an assessment model based on open-ended questions designed to encourage exploration and discovery. Translate these statistics to a workforce, and its capability might increase at a rate up to 123 percent faster than the competition. Who wouldn't like to give that a try?

Extending the exercise, imagine that people originally considered unpromotable or topped out receive half of a company's major promotions into new, more challenging positions. Workers formerly considered to be disciplinary problems now become creative, committed, and self-disciplined contributors. The HOTS approach clearly is a very powerful one, from which businesses could learn a great deal. The first step would be simply to learn the value of questions over answers for the purpose of creating learning and development in businesses and businesspeople.[22]

RESOURCING AT DUPONT

DuPont initiated its developmental approach to change in engineering, where the feedback program had been launched. Klinge still sought to provide guidance, although he admitted to being nervous. In a sense, it seemed "unengineering-like" to have so much open-ended development, but the successful track records at other companies were too good to ignore. The following story illustrates the level of reward that the new approach achieved for DuPont.

Ralph Sims, a chemical engineer with a doctoral degree, was just a couple of years from retirement and always longed to see a solution to the "Freon problem." Freon□, a commonly used fluorocarbon refrigerant and aerosol propellant, was burning a hole in the ozone layer of Earth's atmosphere.[23] At the same time, nearly every nation on the planet demanded more Freon. We were on a collision course with planetary disaster.

The industry had known this for a long time but had not had the focus (or perhaps the confidence) to take it on as an innovation challenge. DuPont's version of Freon was a high margin product representing a large percentage of one division's revenues every year and a huge money maker for the company. Ralph's idea for replacing it put at risk the goose that laid golden eggs.

With a bit of fanfare, Sims cut a deal with DuPont's board of directors, its head of intermediate chemicals, and Green Peace, which had been pressuring DuPont to solve this urgent problem: He committed himself to finding an alternative means of refrigeration. And he promised that the result would result in better outcomes for both the planet and the company.

Sims gathered a resource team that included operators, distributors, and the industrial manufacturers of refrigerators. They included several team members from China and India, whose rapid growth created pressure for a domestically produced toxic refrigerant in order to bypass the more expensive proprietary product. (At the time, that would have accelerated the environmental problem given their technology levels and lower environmental standards.) Sims's three-year development plan was extensive and too technical to describe here but its overarching objectives were to:

- *Find less harmful, more effective alternatives to Freon*
- *Deliver benefits to China and India in exchange for cooperation*
- *Maintain and grow DuPont's earnings over time*

One of the resource team's primary functions was to ask questions that would expose unexamined challenges in order to: 1) help determine the best path forward to a cooperative venture, 2) organize the funding necessary for research, 3) create some internal and external functions, and 4) develop each of the people involved in the initiative so they would be more technically and personally able (in general, better businesspeople) to work on the difficult challenges that might arise as the shift was made to an alternative refrigerant.

The team met monthly and developed many different roles among its members: Technical, financial, internal relations, partnership management, and cultural values. Each meeting began with questions that had to be answered to keep the team on track. One set of those questions was always directed to Sims, in his role as manager for timeliness, budget, and progress toward his core objectives—in other words, the promises he had made to DuPont's board and business unit leaders.

Other questions were designed to help guide his reflection on his personal evolution. Where did he feel that he was tripping himself up? Where had he surprised himself with the advances he and the team were making? The expectation of these diverse, multilayered questions inspired Sims each month, and he often asked people to work with him on finding answers and assessing them. The personal questions, though, were always pushed back to him to examine for himself, and he was encouraged to use them to set aims for his own growth over the next month or the longer term.

Sims's team trusted him to find the truth in himself through reflection. There were no rhetorical questions; all were based on the original plan or the ever-evolving version of it, which meant that Sims was fully responsible for leading the endeavor. As a result, he was much harder on himself than he would have been with any feedback from the former program. And his resistance, when it arose, was always only with himself.

Sims would sometimes privately ask other team members if they had different perspectives, and sometimes they did. But resource team members did not give him any answers to their questions, and those who shared their perspectives were not attached to Sims's adoption of them or not. Different perspectives were viewed as personal reflections, not as competitors for the most accurate, objective assessment. They were just additional ways of looking at things—not truths to be adopted and worked on, as they had been in the earlier feedback processes.

In the end, this innovative project led to world-changing outcomes, as did many other projects taken on by that business group. In accord with the original objectives, they created an environmentally safer substitute for Freon that was lauded by Green Peace and benefitted the entire international community. The move to the new chemical refrigerant took less than two years and became part of the foundation for designing the United Nations Global Compact.

Six years after DuPont's decision to become a developmental organization, Klinge said, "This means no energy is lost on managing people's behavior. You just keep improving their capacity to manage and lead themselves." Even after retirement, both Klinge and Sims worked as human resources consultants to other companies because they witnessed the power of the developmental approach firsthand.

In a developmental organization, the role of resource is often held by individuals previously called supervisors. Resourcing by teams skilled in the Socratic method makes self-management possible across an organization. They may still guide with their expertise but instead of instructing, evaluating, and critiquing with feedback, they use great questions to help individuals and teams develop critical thinking skills and their intrinsic self-managing capacities to make innovative, beneficial contributions to stakeholders.

In the case of Dupont, the group selected five resources from people who volunteered to become proficient at Socratic questioning. It requires learning the philosophy, working with the principles, engaging in real-time thinking, and reflecting on the evolution of oneself as a resource. In particular, those learning to be capable resources observe the evolution of those they resource and see in themselves new levels of courage and wisdom about how to do business.

A key instrument in this process is the explicit shared use of living systems frameworks, which are critical to the resourcing role. Most people have mental models in their heads that predefine paths and outcomes. Sometimes these are externalized and held up as models or steps in assessing progress towards specified ends.

Frameworks offer no answers. Instead, they provide infrastructures that enable any two people or groups to establish a shared language for expressing ideas and developing thinking. Frameworks lead to ideation, innovation, and reflection that invites people to release their useless mental models. They also enable creativity and instill fairness because they are shared and explicit.

Businesspeople learning to be resources attend regular, dedicated learning events with a community of resources from multiple companies. They engage with and are themselves resourced by other businesspeople and educators who are further down the path. The nature of this work has been laid out in other places, including *The Responsible Entrepreneur: Four Game-Changing Archetypes for Founders, Leaders, and Impact Investors.*[24]

Chapter 13

Premise 5: Projection Inevitably Limits and Corrupts Feedback Processes

Individuals without mature inner thoughts and emotions tend to offer feedback based on their dysfunctional worldviews rather than any reality they see outside of themselves. When groups come together to provide feedback on other groups, they tend to unwittingly collude to offer projections shaped by one (or more) dominant personality or based on confusing jumbles of unreliable opinions. In addition, because of the way our minds work, most often feedback results in maximization of a part or an element instead of optimization of the whole, and this inevitably leads to runaway. For this reason, in any situation where reflections on behavior are shared, it is essential to develop processes to overcome the almost universal tendency toward personal projection.

The human tendency toward projection is cogently described in the form of an old Æsop's fable, which tells how each of us carries two heavy bags, one on our back and one on our front. We cannot see the bag on our back, which is full of our own limitations and defects. We easily see the one in front, which contains the defects of others. Sometimes we move the bag on our back around to the front and think we are looking at the defects of others, when really we are looking at our own. We do not always know which bag is where.

Frequently, people in therapy are asked to describe the faults they see in others or the changes they think others should make as a way for their psychologists to understand them through their projections. Without development, we tend to have very limited skills of self-reflection, and so it is difficult to see faults in ourselves. Self-reflection is one of our least developed capabilities, and this factor may cause feedback to be biased in ways that damage team and cross-functional processes. At the very least, not including self-reflection with feedback limits the potential we wish to develop in our organizations.

Projection in Feedback Processes

All projection is a defense mechanism by which individuals attribute characteristics they find unacceptable in themselves to one or more others. Its emergence and manifestation are almost completely invisible—usually we cannot be certain that we actually see it. Consider, for instance, a husband who is consistently hostile but attributes this hostility to his wife, claiming that she is the one with an anger management problem.

A general way of understanding how projection affects feedback, offered by a friend of mine, is based on the "Schrödinger's cat" thought experiment. In 1935, Austrian physicist Erwin Schrödinger created the experiment to illustrate what he saw as a problem with the application of quantum mechanics to everyday objects. He posited a situation in which a cat was put into a sealed, opaque box with a bowl of poisoned food. An observer was asked to determine—without looking into the box—whether the cat had eaten the food and died or sniffed out the poison, refused to eat the food, and survived.

For my purpose here, let's change the focus of the experiment to the effect of the question on the observer. Inevitably, a person without the option to open the box and make a direct observation would begin to construct a possible answer based on information that was not actually available to them. They would tell themself a story that might be based on notions of probability, generalized knowledge about cat behavior, personal experiences of cats, wishful thinking, or any of a myriad of other sources of information. Their efforts would very probably be driven by a desire to crack the puzzle in order to appear smart, funny, or otherwise on top of the question. But in fact, the only way to know *with certainty* whether the cat is alive or dead is to open the box and make a direct observation. An answer based on anything else is only a projection from the mind of the observer, even if it seems to be information coming from within the sealed box and appears to bear on the question.

We do this to people as well. We put them in a box and play out mental experiments that explain their behavior and intentions based on ideas already in our minds, without anything approaching actual information. In real-life settings, serious problems arise when we hold tenaciously to ideas formed about whoever is in the box without testing them against direct observation—in other words, without engaging them independently of our preconceived and unexamined notions.

A version of this experiment was conducted with schoolteachers who were given what they were told were their students' IQ test scores but were actually their locker numbers. Children with low locker numbers got very little help based on the assumption by their teachers that they could not do better. Teachers quickly judged them as less able, and they persisted in this idea and reported it to others even after they were told of the experiment.

This study and many others like it confirm that projection is a particularly insidious and widespread inner process. It relies on assumptions that we construct based on incomplete or false information and uses them as the filters through which we observe people and assess their behavior. Left in place, it inevitably results in failure to discern the truth of individuals: who they are, what they are capable of, and what motivates them.

Maximization Caused by Feedback

A particular kind of maximization that often results from projection is rarely taken into consideration by organizations that rely on feedback programs. That is the lasting effect created when one person, particularly someone with authority, tells another person that there is a problem endemic to their nature or behavior. The person who receives this negative suggestion or judgement rarely contextualizes it within the whole of what has been offered to them as feedback. Nor do they simply reject or ignore it. Instead, they ruminate on it, build cases to defend themself against it, dramatize it out of all proportion, or use it to beat themself up. This is particularly true if the person received similar suggestions or judgments in childhood. Psychologists call this the "tape in our head." It plays in a loop, invading a person's life, and controlling their consciousness.

By its nature, feedback based on projection causes maximization by generating this penetrating inner dialogue with only a part or element of what was offered. This works directly against optimization of the whole, making a person temporarily oblivious of their world, and everything available to them when it comes to assessing their behavior and its effects on others. The loop can run for days, and this is mental runaway.

Sources and Causes of Projection

How is it that people, who would never intentionally deceive themselves, become convinced that what is not actually in front of them is real and that their observations based on these illusions are valid? David Bohm, the Nobel Prize-winning physicist had a useful explanation for how this happens. Based on his research, he suggested that we need to learn to differentiate between *thought* and *thinking* in order to distinguish what is unreal or distorted from what is real and clearly seen. Thoughts are made up of ideas that we hold in memory from past experiences, repeated many times or introduced in highly emotional ways. They hold a strong place in our mental processing, so much so that they shut out any ideas that might provide other ways of looking at current situations.

Bohm described thought as very active, participating in the interpretation of current events and at the same time constantly referring back to preset interpretations. Thoughts do not tell us how things actually are in the present, instead they relate to the current situation based on conclusions that were drawn in the past from situations of a similar nature—in other words, they are projecting the past onto the present. Although we may be expending a great deal of energy and giving our imaginations a good workout, we are not thinking when we busy ourselves with ceaselessly proliferating thoughts.

Similarly, Bohm pointed out, we rarely *feel*. We simply rehash feelings that are part of our recorded history. Old thoughts and feelings are stored in neural networks in our brains and can be triggered whenever anything remotely familiar appears in our field of experience. Moment to moment, without our awareness, old thoughts and feelings intrude on new experiences, falsely interpreting them, closing off new ideas that might challenge or conflict with what we believe we know already.

If left unresolved, this phenomenon can result in many negative effects but we have other options. Learning to observe and understand the process of shifting from thought to thinking is fundamental to developing self-accountability and the capability to ask Socratic questions that can enable change in ourselves and others.

PERSONAL EXPERIMENT

It is possible to test the idea of projection by making yourself the subject of a simple, three-part experiment. Here are the steps:

- Think of a person who annoys you. Spend a moment or two calling their image into your mind.

- List in some detail their annoying behaviors and why they are annoying. Be as specific as possible in order to make your feelings about this person concrete and evident.
- Now make a photocopy of what you have written. Replace this person's name everywhere it occurs with your own, and if necessary, change the pronouns to match your gender. Note that it may take you a day or two (or longer) to develop the necessary nonjudgmental attitude for this experiment. But if you can be really honest with yourself (and it may not be easy), you will find this an eye-opening experience.

———————

It should be clear by now that it is simply impossible to control for the effects of projection in feedback programs. That is the primary and most practical reason for replacing them with something that works.

Chapter 14

Premise 6: Beneficial, Lasting Change Is a Holistic Process

The behavior of a part within a system is the result of the interconnected patterns in the whole system. Consequently, the whole must be considered when one is working to change or correct any apparently independent part, including a person. It is not effective to isolate an individual element (a person or a team) when attempting to change or improve a system. An example is isolating a person who appears to have a discipline problem and working to "fix" them without considering other "systems" relationships that may need to be taken into consideration and developed at the same time.

Most companies have instituted a system called *rating and ranking, which* has a strong connection to the toxicity of feedback when it is used to improve or correct the behaviors of individuals in a system. When we grade on a curve (which is essentially rating and ranking), we assume that some people are likely to pull the entire system down and that it is important to identify and remove them. We also assume that a special few will lift the system to success. In this scheme, managers work to move their people upward on the curve by a variety of means. Each is assessed with an eye to the reasons they are not performing optimally and what they need to do to improve.

Renewed Strategic Direction at Orchard Supply

Let's take as our next example what happened with Lowe's Hardware and Home Improvement (and Sears before them). When I began working with them, they had immersed their Orchard Supply Neighborhood Stores in two systems: Feedback and ranking and rating. Matthew, a recently promoted operations manager, was busy identifying people at the bottom of the scale who were expected to remain there unless something changed. He set out to provide clear feedback to each person, documenting behaviors that did not match the core competencies of the organization. He also offered intense training, coaching, and confrontation sessions based on what each person appeared to need.

Matthew proudly pointed out that his approach was customized, not one of the generic ones he had heard me caution against. To this he added, "Dead wood can cause fires." I learned later that this was his mantra. He meant that people who were "not on the upper curve" undermined others and the organization's ability to get a big boost in a particularly tough industry, where survival required radical differentiation. Orchard needed to become *the* place where people loved to shop, or it would die along with other declining competitors.

I introduced the idea that Orchard's work system, itself—its work design and how it organized people, its business focus, and its performance measurements—might be the primary source of the negative outcomes they were getting, not the individual workers. Matthew's jaw dropped. He frowned and said, "You mean we should mollycoddle them?" This was a phrase I had not heard for years but I got the image quickly.

"No," I said, "we stop blaming them and try to fix them one by one. We work on creating conditions in which each individual not only succeeds but becomes a source of innovation for the business. Then you'll see people at the bottom of the curve change radically and profoundly."

I went on to suggest that Matthew and his fellow managers stop blaming individuals and instead look to the company's current principles, practices, structures, and processes. These were undermining people's ability to experience personal realization in their jobs, and this was true for almost all of the people at the bottom of the curve. A few individuals were thriving, but a company needs all of its people, and you cannot just hire and fire until you get the teams you need. You have to develop everyone, top to bottom, and create a developmental infrastructure that works for each and all. This is the fastest, surest way to change things in any business for the best. And it includes getting rid of all toxic practices, including feedback, core competencies, and rating and ranking, among the dozens of others.[25]

For example, Oscar, one of the employees on Matthew's hit list, had been with Orchard for more than 15 years and was promoted by previous management to the position of lead salesperson. Most of the current leadership team agreed that he no longer met the core competencies required by the job. (It is amazing how different leadership and goals can cause a person to be seen so differently!) They said he took too long speaking to customers and produced too few sales and checkouts from each interaction. The system measured him based on the Proudfoot practice of establishing optimal per-customer interaction times and monthly sales goals.[26]

At the time, Lara Lee was president of Orchard. A few years earlier, she had been central to the leadership team that turned Harley-Davidson around, guided by the principle of locating measures for success in customers' interactions with salespeople and experiences with products. We carried that idea a bit further at Orchard. We wanted its prominent measures to be based not only on customers' experiences of services and products but also on the impacts on their lives each time they engaged with Orchard's people. The goal was to improve customers' lives with *every* interaction.

And it worked. Orchard customers came to count on its salespeople, and the *store team*, as their *life design* team. Sometimes a sale would follow one quick stop at the store, but many times customers returned to consult with salespeople whom they saw as helpful neighbors with insight into what had the potential to make life better. This ongoing, friendly interaction became the business's new strategic direction.

The idea was that if a salesperson or store team came to understand a customer's life and their particular way of engaging in the world (and making purchases), then they could offer genuinely useful suggestions. These helpful suggestions would create a bigger *market basket* sale, which might occur over a series of visits. Developing salespersons to be dedicated, insightful neighbors, with time to spend on customer interactions, would build long-term, friendly customers who would turn to Orchard for more and more life improvements.

This idea, unique in the industry, had been Orchard's founding inspiration. As such, it was its core essence. When it was reidentified, the sales process evolved from quick, turnaround transaction to a series of ongoing interactions to fill customers' needs and make their lives better. The representative metaphor was of neighborly exchanges over the backyard hedge with a wise and helpful neighbor.

Oscar's unique capabilities began to shine once this strategy was embedded in the workforce. He was a natural at looking deeply into people's lives and inventing ideas for them that were thrilling and fulfilling. Customers came to talk with him more and more often, and this time spent with customers was not the negative metric by which his work was measured. His sales soared, and he became a *great* lead salesperson, setting the tone and demonstrating the rightness of the business's strategic direction.

More importantly, as the new work design unfolded, Oscar took on a resource role in relationship with others learning to act like good neighbors to their customers. People reported really liking their customers and genuinely valuing them. Even Matthew, the young manager, admitted that he, too, enjoyed supporting people this way. The new design for ways all of the business's people could contribute, the ways they organized their work, and the roles they took on were the key. Matthew struggled but it felt right to him, and he realized that the nature of feedback caused people to be written off. He also saw that if these same people were not required to meet generic standards, their unique ways of working would become central to Orchard's future. This was the biggest shock resulting from the change initiative, not only for Matthew, but for all of Orchard's managers and executives.

WHAT IS THE THEORY THAT EXPLAINS HOW THIS WORKED?

Cybernetics theorists discovered that even working with artificial intelligence they had to give up the notion of linear cause-and-effect, which posits that one action directly causes one effect. In the nonmechanical world of human life, the cause of any effect is many (often uncountable) interacting elements occurring simultaneously. To change an ongoing effect, most or all of the predominant causes must be engaged in an interactive way.

When we attempt to work with purely linear cause-and-effect in the interactive human world, we are using a model of science proven to be vastly incomplete. To change any single element of a system, we have to consider the dynamics of the whole and work in holistic ways. This view enables us to design change from an integrated perspective; at the same time, it requires that we let go of the false security of programs that focus on specific functions, classes of people, and classes of problems. Isolated measures, such as fixing individuals with behavior problems, must give way to whole-systems measures, which track the overall progress of the system without specifying a particular cause. With any other approach, we invite individuals, systems, and functions into runaway, with the risk of sub-optimizing the whole.

One of the best ways to look at what appears to be a problem person or set of problem behaviors is as an early warning that broad changes are required in the overall system. The working of the organization as a whole is producing problems, and current leadership processes are keeping them in place.

Organizations that work developmentally have found that some individuals are more sensitive to the effects of dysfunctional organizational systems and processes than others, perhaps because they or their families happen to be more open and expressive in relationships with others. Regardless of susceptibility, if instead of punishing these individuals or seeking to get them back on track, we bring them into developmental processes (and redesign work processes, systems, and structures to foster development), then we invite and evoke changes that prevent escalating problems. This starts with assessing where in the system changes are needed and giving people the means to develop understanding of how they can work differently and contribute in ways that are deeply meaningful to themselves and others.[27]

Sometimes, part of the system breakdown that needs addressing is at home. As most businesses know, an employee's home life will inevitably affect their work. It takes a very different kind of behavioral evaluation to extend beneficial change beyond the immediate work environment into an individual's whole life, one that views people as active living organisms. This approach understands that any individual is continuously attempting to develop and contribute their potential. If they have become a problem, it is only because they do not have the capability or the opportunity to engage in a developmental process, and as a result, have gone into mental runaway and are unable to stop worrying about how they are failing or letting people down. This is especially likely in instances when the larger system that they are part of is itself blocking such opportunities.

AN EXAMPLE OF PERSONAL DEVELOPMENT AT KINGSFORD CHARCOAL

It was at Kingsford Charcoal that I met Maria, a single mom with three children who showed up late to work several times a week. Most businesses would have docked her pay, written her up, and eventually fired her. But her base team asked the people development resource team to help them think about how to proceed differently. The resource team asked if the problem might be one of language difficulty. Was English her second language? Her base team confirmed that this might be the case. But the problem was not speaking and understanding spoken English; it really was more about Maria's difficulty reading and writing in English.

Three colleagues met with Maria and made some startling discoveries. After assuring Maria that she would not be fired, that they wanted to make Kingsford a good place for her to work, she admitted that she was illiterate. Because her job required very little reading, she had been very successful until the number of "computer only" memos, training, and instruction increased. Also, her children had trouble at school with reading and writing in English, although like Maria, they were fluent in conversation. The team had uncovered the actual, underlying problem.

Maria told them that she was not the only one facing this challenge. When the team enlisted her help setting up a literacy program, they discovered that the illiteracy rate was 10 percent on average across the company. At one facility, 50 percent of the employees could not read and write. Many clever compensating measures kept this fact hidden, but Maria's family challenges had kept her out of the circles formed for mutual help. All of these employees' children also struggled with reading and writing. They were failing, and this was creating another generation of smart, creative, illiterate people who would need to learn ways to compensate in order to survive in the world.

At Maria's facility, the team set out to remedy what was a national, systemic problem in their own backyard. They hired a part-time teacher, rented a trailer for use as an onsite classroom, and invited all employees and their families to take classes. Maria became the resource to this process, confronting and cajoling her coworkers until they agreed that they needed help. Sometimes she had to pull them kicking and screaming to the school.

Using standard tests to gauge progress, the Kentucky Department of Education recognized the program's success. Toyota USA, another Kentucky company, honored Kingsford for their effort and became a funder for their school and schools at several other area companies where the same issues were uncovered. The program won several awards over the years, and 92 percent of Kingsford's workers and all of their children passed the state test for functional literacy.

If Kingsford had followed the usual path and assumed that Maria was the problem, given her feedback or punished her into correcting her tardiness, the problem of illiteracy might have stayed hidden and been passed on for many more generations. Instead, the developmental path Kingsford chose changed the course of Maria's life, and ultimately changed that of Kingsford and entire communities. This was a pretty impressive result for a team working on a problem that in most other organizations would simply have gotten someone fired.

PART FIVE

THE DEVELOPMENTAL ALTERNATIVE TO FEEDBACK

CHAPTER 15

NEW MEASURES OF ORGANIZATIONAL SUCCESS FOR WORK DESIGN

Here is a quick restatement of the primary reasons to halt all toxic business practices, starting with feedback:

1. Like feedback, all toxic practices limit the development of the full potential of people by undermining the three core capacities that make us fully human and able to contribute. Feedback in particular focuses people externally to others for approval and reflection, instead of first focusing them internally by engaging them in self-observation and self-reflection.

2. Feedback limits an organization's ability to engage each person in service to its stakeholders and their lives. It tends to focus people on the judgments of others and turns their attention to getting the best reviews from coworkers, supervisors, and managers. It turns their minds toward the potential effects of their actions on themselves, instead of engaging them intrinsically by encouraging reflection about themselves. In businesses, this focus on self versus market innovation has the potential to harm every aspect of the organization. At the very least, it will limit its creative expression.

3. Feedback also undermines democracy by conditioning people to listen to what others think rather than think for themselves and come up with their own best responses to given situations. Feedback discourages people from engaging and voting with their own consciences. It does not build critical thinking skills or the ability to deeply understand how society works. Instead, it teaches individuals to believe in thoughts and ideas based on other people's experiences, and encourages them to follow others' suggestions and advice. Feedback also encourages individuals to believe in their unexamined reactions to emotions transmitted with others' suggestions and advice—precisely the effect fearmongering is designed to elicit.

4. Finally, feedback undermines work on ecosystem health by collapsing the mind to the consideration of smaller wholes—our personal selves and our tribes, what is of use to us and members of our family, and what we consider to be of value to us alone. In the same way that it undermines democracy, feedback undermines the imperative to work at the level of systems as large as Earth and its ecosystems. People think small and watch their own backs, discouraged from taking on the biggest challenges of our time. Feedback also creates inner contradictions in people that will always result in taking the safe path, hoping the bigger challenges will work themselves out. Feedback, in tandem with all of the other toxic practices, diverts us from courage.

These limitations and negative consequences are the foundation against which the humanizing potential of essence realization and the development of the core human capacities are most clearly evident. We have seen already how liberating people to establish internal locus of control, broaden their scope of considering, and exercise personal agency can erase the ill effects of feedback and result in big benefits for individuals and organizations. Now we will transition to developmental processes, the alternatives to feedback and the myriad other toxic practices.

Developmental Processes

What are developmental processes, and what makes them possible? How can they eliminate the organizational effects of feedback and other toxic practices? And how can they be instituted in organizational cultures and practices as the basis for regenerative effects in the world?

Developmental processes increase people's capability and will to grow as autonomous actors and free citizens. They include practices that move individuals toward essence realization and expression, enabling them to create unique, value-adding offerings to their communities. This includes diminishing the control of lesser personality traits, not by focusing on them as intractable problems but by learning to observe them, notice their intermittent and inessential nature, and take back the power they have over us.

One requirement for the success of development at the individual level is that it come to fruition in the world. A business is a great place for organizing personal development, which is one reason we build what are called *developmental organizations*.[28] In order to manifest this development, people need to take on different *roles* than they have in the past.

At most organizations, people fill job descriptions, lists of functional tasks that, for the most part, are the same for everyone with the same job title. Job titles and descriptions are assigned independently of individuals' essences or even their personalities. The hiring process seeks people who fit the job by meeting its functional and (sometimes) attitudinal requirements. People stay in their jobs until they are promoted or laid off, leave for work elsewhere, or retire. Status is associated with titles and job descriptions, independently of the people who fill them.

As I am using the term here, a role is fluid and flexible, and defined by the employee who takes it on. A role may be temporary, ending when some task is complete, or long-term, based on the course of the organization's strategic direction. It is always self-chosen and self-bounded, and clearly in service to meaningful and important contributions. A role is considered a learning and development opportunity, as well as an opportunity to contribute, by the one who creates it, those who serve as their resources, and the organization's leaders.

In a developmental organization, each person positions their unique contribution based on guidelines in the form of specific, important organizational goals. Outcomes, contributions, and processes are drawn up in a written plan in alignment with others' roles and in conjunction with the business strategy. A role is not static and cannot be accomplished or measured in the same way as the performance of tasks defined by a job description. It evolves in conjunction with dynamic changes around it and the evolution of the organization. The status associated with a role depends on its unique, highly regarded contributions that were unlikely to come from any other source.

Members of developmental organizations continuously create roles that match with their essences, enabling the progressive stages of their development, and supporting their organizations' strategic directions. Taking on these roles invites people to cross personal boundaries, overcome hurdles, or achieve the next stages of personal and professional evolutions. Encouraging people to take on different roles over time strengthens them and furthers their development, and it increases the vitality and viability of their organizations, as well.

The real work of personal development is to produce a process that adds increasingly higher levels of value. *Value-adding process* is a term and image borrowed from living systems disciplines, which view work in terms of how it is sourced and what it transforms to add value to the next effort in a workflow. For example, a seed saver and hybridizer works well when she takes into consideration the entire process that her seeds make possible. Do they change the lives of farmers, food processors, chefs, and family cooks for the better? Do they regenerate soils and result in beneficial effects on all of the associated downstream processes? Is it possible for a particular seed variety to vitalize each phase in the entire process from soil and farmer to food processor and market? Is the seed saver/hybridizer envisioning the entire process from Earth and back to Earth and her role in it?

The value-adding view of work is not the same as the value-*added* view, which evokes an economic extraction process. *This difference cannot be stressed strongly enough!* In a value-added process, each person looks to see what they can add to give themself a margin of profit over what they took from an ecosystem or community, or purchased from a supplier. This is a narrow view that considers effects only in terms of the individual's limited experience and expected gain. Value-added work does not take responsibility for the viability and evolution of the entire course of a regenerative progression. By contrast, *value-adding work champions and becomes organically engaged in regeneration and evolution.*

This distinction holds for *everyone* in an organization. In general, each person is responsible for their own self-evolution and for contributions to the evolution of others in their world. Consciously assuming this responsibility elevates a person's will to grow, it makes them interested in personal or professional development, and it enables them to commit to a role through which they can bring value to regenerative processes.

For a role within an organization to be truly developmental, it must be self-managed and driven intrinsically by a person's desire to mature and evolve with the world around them. People in this process recognize activities and outcomes that are of interest and that they want to pursue in the world. They recognize as part of their professional development that they do not understand certain important things as well as they would like and become motivated to gain understanding that will make adding value possible. This leads to greater creativity and the ability to see the potential for adding to the effectiveness of others and their organizations.

For these reasons, in a developmental organization, managers do not send people to classes or training courses as a way to solve their own problems.

Participants may opt to attend but only after thinking about what they want to learn and how they hope to apply it. They go in with the expectation that learning will be employed in the role that they hold in the organization. Without this aspiration, nothing much ever comes of training; it does not in any way help people develop and almost never leads to their taking on greater challenges or new roles.

To benefit from a developmental process, it is important to learn to know the world in a more systemic way. This means elevating our understanding about how things work or how they can be developed. This challenge can at first cause people to feel incomplete and often thoroughly humbled. Such destabilization requires that people employ a developmental mental process to manage their inner dialogues with themselves, individually and in their teams.

A hazard arises when people use the uncomfortable feelings of destabilization as an excuse to back off. They start withdrawing and end up unhappier than they were in the first place; it becomes a struggle for them to maintain on-going efforts to fulfill their potential. This calls for an organizational design that can support their efforts. Once a person sees something in a new way, it usually stays in their mind, and they never really drop out of working on it. Always in this case, it is necessary to observe oneself and do a bit of self-managing in response to fear or other negative mind states—such as anger, embarrassment, or boredom. When the ego is present, it is necessary to work on any feelings of inadequacy. People can be made aware that these are inevitable and temporary reactions, and once aware of their growing capability to observe and manage uncomfortable emotions and negative self-judgment, they can take on destabilization and learn to manage it in a self-appreciating and humorous way.

Krone used to ask his teams and cohorts at Procter & Gamble and those of us in his resourcing sessions to think about Don Quixote as a way to experience the idea of development. Quixote's character is the sort that allows someone to entertain the possibility of ongoing personal development—in other words, to dream impossible dreams. This is an important capacity that all people can build into themselves, and they can dedicate themselves to becoming who they wish to be. They can look at the world and everyone in it this way, adopting Quixote's optimistic and courageous stance toward development, and this will make them better able to take on their own development.

The Quixote attitude is not "out of touch with reality," instead when people maintain goodwill and faith, it tends to enable them to be more and more in touch with reality, defined as how the world actually works and its real potential. The more a person can do this, the better off they will be. It is a way of attacking one's own egoism and sense of inadequacy, and when people transcend those limits, they discover that they and the world are better off than they were before.

Essence

Because all developmental processes are based on essence and the maturation of essence, it is important to know what it is and how to recognize it in people, organizations, and all other living systems. Personal essence is defined as the unchanging aspect of an individual that is experienced by others as their uniqueness. Essence is different than personality, which changes as we learn to adapt ourselves to different environments. Essence can mature over time, particularly in expression, and so it can seem to change. But, in fact, essence is by definition innate and unchangeable.

Most contemporary societies and organizations do not welcome or appreciate essence expression. Culture requires conformity and restrains people from purposefully expressing and becoming aware of their unique inner being. Most people censor their thoughts, which restricts their evolution and narrows their work. The consequence is a terrible and destructive limiting of the potential of humanity, which guarantees that most of us will be far less happy than we could be.

The discovery of essence can be brought about in any one of three ways. First, essence can emerge from the stress to accomplish something or to cross a boundary that previously has not been crossed. Boundary crossing is a challenge that requires exercising and strengthening will, and this almost inevitably causes essence to make itself apparent.

Second, self-observation and reflection over a long period of time, with the intention of developing self-knowledge, can enable a person to recognize and articulate their essence. And third, when the mind is relaxed, images are allowed to emerge that make essence evident. This requires development of the capability to image the working of life and the mind moving through time, expressing itself as it grows.

The stress of crossing a new boundary is different from the kind of stress people experience when an institution or organization constrains them from working at their highest level and doing what they know is right. Destabilization brings forth essence while constraint causes frustration and eventual apathy. This crippling stress is also different from the stress of reaching beyond one's current capabilities and exercising the will to make a contribution in service to something larger than oneself.

As humans, we need to feel that our work is meaningful, valuable, and challenging. A routine job in which we feel unimportant and unable to apply our best selves is one in which we have not been encouraged to express our essence and let our creativity flourish. This is what distinguishes a job for which we are hired or contracted from a role that we have chosen to accept.

Developmental organizations allow people to discover their essences and mature their expression. In return, relating to work from essence enables people to be maximally creative and effective on the job. Some people are naturally attracted to and good at particular kinds of work based on their essences but any kind of work can be approached from essence. There are as many possible approaches to getting a job done as there are essences in the world. A job or role may be routine; the person who takes it on and the essence they convey are always unique, allowing for the potential for creativity and contribution in any position.

Developing and Maturing Essence Expression

Everyone has capacities that they can develop more fully and an open-ended capacity for increased potential. For example, when education is integrated with business and employment in a whole, living system, the system's developers attempt to discover each student's essence. To find roles in which they can be maximally effective and innovative and that align with developing capacities, they ask the following questions:

- *How can we capture the essences of people in our education process?*
- *How can we make each individual more creative and innovative?*
- *How can we create a seamless transition between school and work?*

When working from essence, we discover the processes and activities to which we are easily attuned and find what we are effective at doing. That is when we know we are expressing and maturing what is unique in us. For example, one person feels the need to engage in something that allows her to exercise meticulousness, another needs to care for a larger entity. These are both examples of the *expression* of distinctive essence, although they do not necessarily reveal that essence. Articulating an essence involves discovering it from the inside versus having it defined from the outside. Knowing one's essence is about recognizing "where you feel most you." Practices that undermine this discovery are by definition toxic and must be eliminated from education, and work if human potential is to be developed and realized.

Essence uses personality as a vehicle for expression, and often personality evolves as essence expression becomes fuller or more mature. Every person, when starting from essence, has a unique and creative way of thinking. When innovation and creative thinking are important in a business or other organization, then it is absolutely necessary to build in developmental processes for the expression and evolution of these qualities.

Sometimes it seems that essence changes when, for instance, a person becomes better able to use personality as an instrument to express their essence. Personality is the adaptive side of our being, which is apparent when people retrain themselves to handle challenging situations or change themselves in order to deal with an overwhelming world. In painful or frustrating circumstances, or when we are challenged to become smarter and more creative, the question we need to constantly ask ourselves is not, "Can I *change* who I am?" It is, "Can I *become* who I am?"

Essence is that aspect of a person to which they easily relate and do not typically seek to change. We say, "I feel at one with myself" or "She is true to herself." Such comments suggest that we are aware of a distinct essence, the unconstrained and unlimited aspect of our own or another's inner self.

CHAPTER 16

DESIGNING FOR GROWTH AND DEVELOPMENT

In *The Regenerative Business*, I wrote at length about how to design and construct an organizational work system that provides the fundamental conditions to make essence maturation and the development of core capacities possible. I began by outlining three design criteria that focus on these conditions.

The first criterion, *initiative activation*, is intended to foster the ability of every member of an organization to take initiative with regard to building a world-changing business. The second, *developmental infrastructure*, helps integrate individual initiative and organizational direction in order to achieve mutual success. The third, *change accelerator*, involves orchestrating the conscious dialogue that will ensure that enlightened disruption is actually occurring in the market and society as a whole.

Human creativity tends to become scattered or diffused without a rigorous discipline in place to focus it. These three criteria are specifically designed to enable businesses to provide focus, organization, and order to the initiatives of their members, so that their creative energy gains coherence and thrust. The criteria also provide guidance for the initiation and management of large-scale change. They are applicable to businesses, communities, ecosystems, and nations because they allow groups to start where they are and grow from there. For this reason, I have found them to be contagious. The minute workers begin to experience and master them within the workplace, they start to carry them out into their communities, where they can be put to use to benefit the public.[29]

What can be achieved with developmental work design and management practice cannot be overstated. People are often able to liberate themselves from harmful or otherwise unproductive behavioral patterns in which, as one young employee put it, they feel "as if [their] feet were trapped in cement." She understood the challenges but did not have the ability to work on them. What she heard in feedback from others did not resonate with her, even with all the examples she was given. Once feedback was eliminated, she was able to look more squarely at what she was up against, and this enabled her to see it in realistic proportion and find creative ways to take it on.

Another example is Shelley, who worked as a customer service representative for an Oregon-based market data company. She received feedback that admonished her to become a better listener and understand all of the details of an issue before she shifted into problem-solving mode—a pretty basic skill for an online or telephone service rep. Her feedback team used customer evaluations in an effort to help her see that people sometimes felt she was missing their point and going to work on the wrong thing.

But Shelley was very creative when faced with complex situations. During a developmental plan event, she and others explored the idea of external considering as a basis for evolving the company's approach to customer service. Shelley was inspired by the difference between asking customers to identify their problems and actually connecting with their lives. Up to that time, her team had engaged customers in a fairly conventional manner: ask the customer to describe the problem and make sure you understand it, including any specific information required for a solution.

As part of the company's work to build a developmental organization, Shelley created her own developmental plan. Her aim was to make a real difference for her customers by practicing external considering. What would most benefit each customer? This was a much different activity than accepting feedback from her manager and peers, and slowing down to become a better listener. As part of the work on her plan, Shelley decided to experiment with a shift from question-and-answer to dialogue, seeking to discover the unique circumstances that her customer brought to their buying process. She wanted to understand it as if she was having the same experience. She wanted to put herself in the customer's shoes.

When I later spoke with Shelley, she enthusiastically reported that she had tried the new strategy and worked with a customer who purchased a media marketing program and was having trouble executing it. She became his "thinking partner," working with him to figure out what kind of experience he wanted to provide for his clients, how the media program would be helpful, and how he would measure success.

In the course of their conversation, she and the customer imagined together, creating a shared story that allowed them to see the desired client experience in precise detail. This helped the customer clarify exactly what he wanted and how the marketing program would help him do it. He was deeply grateful for the genuinely meaningful support he received and, not coincidentally, a short time later he also made an additional significant purchase.

I asked Shelley about her experience. She described it as somewhat scary because she had to work in a way that she had heard about in a development session but had no experience of herself. She felt nervous taking it on but she wanted to commit to it as a way to broaden her scope of considering. She brought in an exercise that we had been working on, which involved managing her internal considering by reflecting on herself and her fear of failing. When these fears arose, she addressed them by remembering her aim: To benefit the lives of her customers. This helped her find courage and remain in the dialogue.

Shelley summed it up for her team this way:

"I genuinely understood what it takes to engage with a customer as a unique person, to see where they're coming from in their interactions with other people. I glimpsed a real life, and the person living it mattered to me. This was very different from seeing a person's problem and listening hard to hear the salient details, as if they would help me come up with a magic solution. It took a lot of courage and faith in my own imagination. It was exciting to find out that I could do it, and it was thrilling to hear the customer find his own solution, a true one based on his actual needs."

Shelley's success came from developing the capability to be her customer's thinking partner, not from feedback on her behavior. It sprang from her commitment to imagine the customer's real life, not from following a better script on the phone or online. She could see for herself what was needed. The results were thrilling to hear because the process she had entered with the customer resonated deeply with her own self-development.

An epilogue to Shelley's story is very moving. At the time, her 13-year-old son, Rafael, was behaving in some unexpectedly challenging ways. She realized that her aim for customers could be transferred to her interactions with her son. She wanted to understand his life and be his thinking partner. She knew this was critical to his happiness and success later in life, and to her own as his mother. She stopped herself many times over the next several weeks from offering solutions for his problems based on the ways she was experiencing them. She could also see how her usual way of mothering him was escalating his stress—and her own. He later described the way he had been feeling as, "It was like she was trying to run my life."

Shelley finally pulled out a systemic framework that she used in the program at work, one that invites people to engage from alternative perspectives with the forces at odds in a situation rather than trying to argue them away. She invited Rafael to engage with her in this structured way of thinking, which is part of the developmental process an organization can use to build systemic critical thinking skills.

When frameworks like this one are used on a recurring basis, they help people develop the ability to view situations and experiences from more whole and dynamic perspectives. Coupled with personal self-managing, they enable seeing without judging and help all parties in a difficult situation discover the whole of the potential hidden by our normal way of engaging.

It took a few times but Rafael finally saw that his mother was trying to change her way of helping him—allowing him to articulate his situation and see more than he was seeing, without trying to influence him or persuade him to change his mind or his behavior. Instead of offering Rafael a suggestion, she invited him to work with her side-by-side to make sense of the challenges he faced. After their conversations, he always left with something he wanted to try and a way to guide himself through it. Shelley created a mini-developmental organization that demonstrated the changes she wanted to make in her own life. Rafael felt this and made changes, too.

What Makes Developmental Processes Work?

For any group, regardless of size, all individual members must be self-accountable and self-governing to be viable, vital, and evolving appropriately within the ever-changing world in which they live and work. The developmental process is not a canned program to be installed in any generic organization. It is a way of seeing clearly and working effectively that must be developed. If it is to be effective in the long run, within the contexts of each of their lives, individuals must have stewardship for the welfare of the whole. To self-manage their behaviors, individuals must be aware of them and their impacts on the effort to benefit the lives of others.

This is the fork in the road. Here, those who advocate external feedback as the solution to life's problems take one path, based on the belief that people cannot develop the awareness needed for change. Those who have seen the unlimited potential of a developmental approach based on a holistic, living-systems view take another. This road is of a higher order, in that it is based on a belief that people have the capacity to be *self-managing* once they have learned to be *self-observing* and *self-reflecting.*

To be capable of self-reflection is to be able, of one's own volition, to see oneself in the moment of action, and to regulate and adjust one's behavior while in motion. Everyone has experienced self-reflection on at least a few occasions. The aim is to make it more routine and accessible in all situations. In the developmental version of the human story, one nurtures the capability to be consistently self-reflective through the creation of developmental plans that provide for the required inner work and outer contribution. The plan includes establishing alliances with others who not only have deep familiarity with the self-work involved but also possess the skill and time to serve as resources. This is a Socratic process that involves learning to learn and learning to develop. It is worlds apart from a feedback program; offering feedback as part of a Socratic learning relationship is entirely inappropriate and can derail development.

COLGATE, SOUTH AFRICA

One of life's joys—and usually a tremendous shock—is discovering that a person we thought was stuck forever has made a great change. The best thing about my work is watching this realization dawn on people and seeing it alter the lives of both the observed and the observer. Often this occurs between a manager and an employee, or a parent and their child. All of us have been stuck for far too long in the belief that people are limited from birth, and can only pick up a few new skills and gather a bit more knowledge to add to what they learned in school.

My most profound experience of this realization came in South Africa about 25 years ago. For a long time, black South Africans were forbidden to receive any formal education and were not supported by school systems in their efforts to learn. This was based on the belief that blacks were unable to learn or grow and efforts to educate them were a waste of resources—a racist perspective institutionalized by Afrikaners, the white descendants of Dutch colonizers. When I arrived on the scene, the old order was breaking down, but it was assumed that it would take generations to bring blacks into the modern world.

My opportunity to test the strength of this false assumption came when I was asked by Stelios Tzesos, a Greek national and Colgate Palmolive's general manager in Africa, to help him turn the company around after decades of neglect. At the same time, he wanted to contribute to the forming of the new South Africa. We had one Afrikaner on staff highly resistant to the changes, and he actually left the organization when Tzesos announced the venture. Many other Afrikaners stayed, although most were skeptical of our plans and figured they would be rushing in as heroes when the black employees proved not up to the task.

Adding to the pressure, the new South African constitution mandated that all companies move blacks into the top 5 percent of management positions within five years of its ratification. We had *one* university-educated black member in the entire organization, a PhD chemist who worked in the lab but not in a leadership or managing role. The other approximately 2,990 black employees had never been enrolled in formal educational programs or received any professional certifications. It is not surprising that the Afrikaner leaders, given their paradigm of how intelligence is developed and demonstrated, stood ready to rescue us when we failed.

But we did not fail. As Tzesos kept pointing out, "Lack of education is not the same as lack of intelligence." We engaged a core team of black leaders, a mix from eight tribes, along with Afrikaners in an intense, structured business change process. We taught this team about financial effectiveness and how critical thinking can make any strategic and operational effort innovative.

The blacks' experiences as parents, tribal leaders, and active participants in township governance provided a good real-life basis for understanding how change works and can bring evolution into organizations. We used it to test new ideas.

I often say that I have *never* seen anyone take on this work with as much relish, speed, and love as these black South Africans. I could not keep up with the group as they extrapolated ideas from our approach, testing them on everything from their jobs to their leadership roles in families, tribes, and communities. In a sense, they already had a living-systems way of thinking, unhindered by the fragmented and linear nature of Western intellectual traditions. On the other hand, Colgate's Afrikaner managers had been educated in ways that did not provide them with an understanding of how living systems work. As we made rapid progress, one of these leaders begrudgingly admitted that some kind of magic was happening and made the astute comment that "blacks have less to unlearn."

Just one year later, Nelson Mandela joyfully presented the Constitutional Award to Colgate's new management team—which was now *95 percent black*! The members selected by the team to represent them at the award ceremony pulled two of their previous Afrikaner managers with them onto the stage. These Afrikaners had given up their leadership positions and were now serving as resources to the new team. When we all gathered at headquarters the next morning to share the story of the ceremony, Tzesos asked the representatives why they had dragged the Afrikaners onto the stage with them.

Bheko, a Zulu leader who was now senior operations manager, replied, "because the white leaders have been the bravest of us all, standing by and watching their roles change so radically." Adriaan, one of the Afrikaners who were coaxed onto the stage, listened from the side of the room. Rather sheepishly, he spoke up and said that the biggest challenge for him was watching Bheko. He had managed Bheko for 10 years before the change process began, but he hardly knew him and had little respect for him. In the past year, he noticed how Bheko welcomed him as a resource and showed deep respect for his knowledge: "He was always present and attentive. He understood and tested everything he heard, and he always asked for more," Adriaan said. He spoke emotionally of pride in his ability to watch this change happen, acknowledge it in his own mind, and now to feel humbled by it. We all cheered.

Many Afrikaners and English South Africans did not make that leap. But in retrospect, I would estimate that half of Colgate's Afrikaners did. On the morning after the ceremony, several in that room were smiling and shaking their heads. It is possible to educate people to change. And it is not as hard as you would think.

EVIDENCE FOR A DEVELOPMENTAL ALTERNATIVE

In each of these studies and case stories, a profound shift occurs following the introduction of the developmental approach, usually after an extended period of time. In South Africa, the financial, personal, and community returns were almost immediate. In this case, significant change began to occur within six months, and it did not diminish as time passed. An almost instant about-face occurred among people who previously had little control of their work lives and had as a consequence not connected in meaningful ways to Colgate's offerings.

This resembled my experience with the HOTS program children. In most cases, the three core human capacities do not die but lie dormant. They go into hiding or they are expressed elsewhere than at school or work. Similarly, a person's essence waits to be awakened. Feedback does not kill it, instead it sends it looking for shelter. Even after decades, the opportunities are not lost to discover and express one's essence, and to make important contributions. Lost creative energy can be reignited by discovering and activating the essences of an organization and its people.

Better Is the Enemy of Best

We tend to default to the gratification we get from small improvements, rather than risk the discomfort or destabilization of seeking big changes. In the case of feedback, having some idea of how others see us is better than having no idea why we are being treated a particular way. It is challenging to imagine a more holistic way of working that would take us beyond this single step of improvement. At DuPont, when we tested to see if people could experience the benefits of developmental ways of working versus the former feedback approach, even we were surprised.

Effectiveness was assessed in group discussions and by tracking the financial return to the business before and after toxic practices were abandoned. People were asked if feedback from others gave them a better ability to understand themselves. Before the switch to a developmental, self-directed way of working, the answer was "yes" slightly more than half of the time. One year after the change process was implemented, it was hard to find people who would agree to return to feedback. They felt they could see themselves more clearly after the structured development work, and their new mastery over themselves made them hungry for more. Supervisors welcomed this result; managers and even some team members never liked feedback. They much preferred supporting the growth of people who were self-directed, and they appreciated the profoundly improved return on the development of this skill, which they saw grow year after year.

In the *Harvard Business Review*, Seventh Generation co-founder and former CEO Jeffrey Hollender described tracking 52 companies that moved away from their use of feedback and other toxic practices to adopt developmental processes.[30] The results? Revenue growth improved from 35 to 60 percent, turnover of key people was significantly reduced, and new relationships were forged with giant distributors such as Whole Foods and Babies "R" Us. The supply system also steadily improved, and a few suppliers participated in developmental sessions with Seventh Generation employees. The primary means of transfer had come from company employees who changed how they worked with their contractors. Their courage to initiate and guide change was considerably more powerful when tied to their desire to make contributions rather than to internal satisfaction derived from feedback.

Chapter 17

What Do We Need in Order to Work Developmentally?

How will we create organizations that are never compelled to resort to feedback and other toxic practices? I will begin my answer to this question with a review of the six premises and a short demonstration of the ways they are related as a whole.

Premise 1: Self-Governing Behavior is Energy Effective. If you honestly believe that people can learn to be self-governing, you will no longer try to govern them by influencing or persuading them of your view. Every time you see something that needs changing in another person, you will work on yourself first to avoid projecting what belongs to you and to examine biases you likely bring to your judgments. Your focus will shift from people's problems to ways in which you can be a resource to their development opportunities.

Premise 2: Self-Reflective Capability Is Necessary for Self-Governance. When you have understood the potential that self-reflection has for fostering self-governance, you will find time to include it in every event. You will also use systemic frameworks to make self-reflection more effective. Self-reflection will build your own and others' capability, and it is good for the organization and all the people in it. It is easy, once you have practiced it for a while, to discern that working without self-reflection is toxic to everyone's growth.

Premise 3: The Basis of Self-Reflection and Self-Governance Is a Developmental Plan. To become the power process for building change and growth into an organization, development needs to be ritualized. A developmental plan for everyone in the organization puts their growth back into their hands. The foundations of these plans are significant contributions their owners wish to make to the organization's stakeholders. They include an ongoing self-reflection and evolution process.

Premise 4: Self-Observation and Resourcing Develop Self-Reflection. The only nontoxic alternative to feedback is self-observation and self-reflection, which are enabled by skillful resourcing based on the Socratic method. A resource's role derives from the meaning of the term *resource*—to return another to themselves as a source. An individual is the only source of their own reflective discoveries and developmental paths, and of the personal agency required to act on their plan over time.

Premise 5: Projection Inevitably Limits and Corrupts Feedback Processes. This premise reminds us how much opportunity exists to see firsthand how feedback nurtures all the wrong things in people. It activates and accelerates biases of all kinds and includes no built-in process for self-examination. When everyone is turned toward self-reflection and self-governing, then the activation of such biases is eliminated. We see ourselves in our internal mirrors, never in other people's gaps and flaws. In this way, we become self-governing agents, invited to express our own essences, and reflect on their evolution as it unfolds.

Premise 6: Beneficial, Lasting Change Is a Holistic Process. This premise overarches the entire activity of development. It creates a pervasive philosophy and technology that makes developmental organization a way of life. This is what it means to be regenerative. Feedback is only one of dozens of practices whose toxicity is illuminated by the commitment to change as a holistic process.

SET A DEVELOPMENTAL PLAN

These are the basic steps for creating an organizational developmental plan:

1. Take stock of the sources of your practices. Question your assumptions about how people work. Look at the worldviews behind your programs. Learn more about the business and organizational practices that are most toxic to developing and realizing human potential. Give your business a real return on its people.

2. Create a new charter for working with people. Avoid platitudes. The key to shifting to developmental organization is to engage people by directing work toward what they want to contribute to in the market—a customer, stakeholder, or planetary imperative. They will hear and be resourced by the imperative and, if they are given scope to develop, they will make the necessary changes to realize it.

3. Design work systems that support the development of everyone in the organization. Initiate personal development, the development of critical thinking skills, and a whole-systems perspective.

4. Create an image of what is possible for your organization. Consult *The Regenerative Business* and adapt the five evolutionary phases to your situation. Energetically and systemically develop your own leadership capabilities and those of others in your organization.[31] Connect to a larger developmental community (see some suggestions below on page X).

TURN THE CORNER ON FEEDBACK

Let's return to the story of Casandra, the Silicon Valley human resources manager from Chapter 8. She discovered that the feedback program her company purchased from Franklin Covey was not producing the promised benefits, contrary to the testimonials. In particular, there were many downsides or side effects, and the desired business improvement had not been realized. After eight years, she decided to make an extensive evaluation of the program. She pulled together one of her characteristic focus groups, a set of people who had been engaged in the process for six months to eight years. The group reflected the entire organization, both functionally and in terms of perspective.

Casandra and the focus group assessed all of the company's human resource programs, starting with feedback. In less than two days, they were clear not only why feedback was unpopular, but also why it did not work and harmed the company, its people, and society at large.

Their summary report included the following assessments:

1. The majority of people in the group felt less self-directed than when they were new employees at the company, given freedom to contribute in meaningful ways.

2. Managers felt no better about handling their tough cases. In spite of extensive training and coaching, some had not shaken their attitudes toward particular individuals and others were not able to trust their own assessments.

3. People were not seeing changes in the behavior of feedback recipients. In fact, feedback for improvement seemed to have a negative effect on self-efficacy. This led almost without exception to poorer performance and no change in behavior.

4. Praise had the same effect. It did not improve performance or provide incentive to excel beyond the current level. However, it did seem to move subordinates to seek more praise and bring their successes to managers.

5. Coaching in one-shot sessions seemed to make little difference—not due to lack of interest but from lack of clarity or understanding of how to proceed over time.

6. Coaching did change behavior and performance when it came from manager to subordinate by setting a direction for change.

Casandra concluded that no one favored the feedback process or wanted to be involved. It was evident that feedback had little positive effect on either the giver or the receiver.

I passed along to Casandra a set of articles published in a 1965 issue of the *Harvard Business Review*.[32] They were a report on research at General Electric, undertaken in response to an earlier HRB article, "An Uneasy Look a Performance Appraisal," by Douglas McGregor, known for his Theory X and Theory Y ideas about management styles.[33] The authors, three highly respected psychologists employed by General Electric, had documented much the same results of feedback-based processes that Casandra's team found 40 years later.

The most important take-away from Casandra's survey and the research reported in the HBR articles may be that organizations rarely pay enough attention to academic research and to employees when they push back on programs. They follow the lines of consultants who promise a new program or best practice every other year or so, and they rely on testimonials as the sole means of assessing their value instead of questioning the assumptions or premises on which they are founded.

GUIDELINES FOR EVOLVING PEOPLE

The critical thinking necessary for accurately interpreting other people's behavior—in terms of meaning, intention, and external effect—is the same skill needed to accurately interpret one's own. Critical thinking includes the ability to observe inner processes and do so accurately; it is our means of recognizing and understanding the source of decisions, actions, and reactions, including our own.

For this reason, in order to accurately interpret others' behaviors, we must develop rigorous and precise self-observing and self-remembering capability, along with critical thinking as a way to manage our perceptions. In particular, we must learn to observe our thinking as it occurs without assuming that it is accurate because it is all we see. Perceiving is not neutral and unaffected by our internal conditioning. That is, we do not necessarily understand our thought process, how it frames our thoughts, and why we're thinking what we're thinking in the first place. We may not have the ability to catch our automatic thinking moment to moment as it arises. We may not have access to its sources. We may not notice that our biases are blinding us, that we are deeply attached to many false interpretations of reality, and that we operate from assumptions formed in this mental fog. That's the bad news.

The good news is that, with strong dedication to practicing self-observing, self-remembering, and critical thinking all of us are able to clear our minds in order to understand ourselves and others. This is the basis for reliable, objective self-assessment and for resourcing the self-assessment of others. It also enables us to gauge the accuracy of others' perceptions and interpretations while protecting us from adopting their thoughts without proper examination. These skills are needed in all aspects of our lives. And it is because we must develop them that we also must stop relying on feedback and instead build capacity in people throughout all of our businesses and other organizations.

Our current theories about the ways perception, interpretation, and understanding work are based on the mistaken impression that we can make feedback accurate and fair by designing out bias, false interpretation, and misunderstanding—simply by giving people a new set of steps. But you cannot eliminate the effects of external influence (social perception) and internal biases. Self-management, clear perception, and critical thinking are *ableness*, as such, they must be developed over many years through the practice of observing our own and others' minds at work. Ableness is the stuff of spiritual development in lineage traditions (such as meditation and internal reflection) that was excluded from the study of psychology by Watson and from behavioral psychology today. This bifurcated understanding of reality and the human mind has yet to be repaired.

The Practice that Makes Great Mental Skills Possible

I suggest the following four practices as ways to make it possible for every person to develop ableness for the developmental alternative to feedback:

1. **Reflection:** Introduce the idea of reflecting as a way of life and work. Post questions at recurring intervals, such as transitions between parts of the day and/or the beginnings and ends of development sessions and events. Questions are intended to evoke self-reflection on how people are processing the world around them. When it is done honestly and repeatedly, this work builds the inner guide or compass necessary for self-awareness and self-understanding, nurturing our capacity for self-management.

2. **Frameworks:** Use whole systems frameworks to guide individual and collaborative thinking. Reflection is easier and more effective when mental frameworks are used to help reframe *how* one thinks about a subject or decision. They make thinking more complete and integrate it more fully into the whole of one's experience. We all have ways of organizing our thinking and patterns for understanding experience that are largely invisible and automated. These need to be brought into consciousness, examined, and discarded or improved if they are not serving us well.

    Working with frameworks to accelerate critical thinking skills is a foundation process for enabling all people in an organization to see themselves clearly, including their roles, effects on others, and responsibility to advance endeavors. In turn, this enables them to connect to the organization's overall strategy by imaging it at work, perceiving more of what is happening around them, and taking on bigger challenges.

3.   DEVELOPMENTAL ENGAGEMENT: Support each person in the organization in their efforts to reveal and express their potential in the context of the business strategy. Eight processes guide resourcing ourselves and others developmentally:

   a)   ENGAGE PEOPLE, NOT HIERARCHIES. Make all interactions self-to-self, placing both people on the same level. Each is the equal of the other, engaging with ideas that are exchanged without hierarchy. In these engagements, no one has power or authority over another.

   b)   IMAGE LIFE *WORKING*. Help people image the working of life and systems, seeing events and situations (and the people involved in them) as dynamic and alive, rather than static or fragmentary. This is probably the most effective way to help people overcome their fixed views of others.

   c)   START FROM ESSENCE AND POTENTIAL. Whenever you notice yourself seeing others as problems, switch to seeing them instead as essences to be engaged and potentials to be developed.

   d)   REFLECT! REFLECT! REFLECT! Always invite reflection on self- and group processes as a way to bring inner and outer work together.

   e)   DEVELOP A SHARED LANGUAGE AND SHARED PROCESSES. Using frameworks, ask questions that evoke thoughtful discernment so that authority and control are shared.

   f)   SUPPORT PERSONAL EVOLUTION. When you commit to resourcing someone's development, engage with them from a place of genuine caring. Eliminate toxic practices, such as correcting behavior or speech or offering advice. Replace them with developmental practices such as destabilization and the use of thought-provoking restraints.

g) **ARTICULATE PERSONAL AND ORGANIZATIONAL AIMS.** At the end of every developmental engagement, leave people (including yourself) with an aim that provides direction for evolution.

h) **EVOLVE ESSENCE.** Design engagements that allow people to discover and express essence by encouraging them to initiate from personal agency. Essence always answers when given freedom.

4. **PRINCIPLES AND PREMISES:** The development of managing principles—coupled with a clear, profound, and compelling strategic direction—provides overarching guidance to supplant criteria based on competencies for managing and aligning organizations. No organization can cover all of the areas in which competencies will be needed or guide people to achieve them with feedback. Managing principles provide coherent and effective behavioral guidance for all organizational members. When coupled with the three preceding developmental guidelines, they lift up aspirations for personal development and contribution.

Strategic direction is built on the unique essence of the organization, as well as its social and ecological imperatives, and the market position that it can own. When these are articulated as a formal strategic corporate direction with which everyone associated with the company is encouraged to engage, they become the guiding light for all of the organization's persons, teams, and functions.

Conclusion

Coming to terms with practices that are toxic is more than a debate about what works best for business results. That question does matter, and answering it gives businesses the foundation to make the transition worth doing. But there are more important reasons than financial rewards that hold sway. The highest success in any kind of activity—from child rearing and education to business and governance to ecosystems regeneration and spiritual practice—comes from seeing every person as unique and capable of participating in the evolution of systems and programs.

Reasons for Development Beyond Financial Payoff

These are the three most important reasons for an organization to transition from toxic practices to developmental processes:

First, to create a society that works effectively. For society to work, each of us must cultivate a strong sense of personal responsibility for the impact of our own actions on the world. We must learn to feel our connection to all other people and understand that our lives are interdependent. Becoming solipsistic, which is the tendency in many situations, leaves us asking only, "What's in it for me?" Most business practices, like most organizational practices in general, invite solipsism, and this is how it gets built into organizational cultures and work design.

But what if we imagine every organization redesigning work and capability building to foster the three core human capacities: Locus of control, scope of considering, and source of agency? This effort requires the removal of all undermining toxic practices, and feedback is the logical place to start. It is one of the oldest of our modern processes for managing human interactions, and as such it is embedded in many others. Changing this one toxic practice has the potential to transform performance reviews, training and development, and all of the ways teams work together, among hundreds of other day-to-day practices.

SECOND, TO ACHIEVE FULL HUMAN POTENTIAL. The phrase "to achieve my full potential" has come to be a platitude of the worst order. But policy, governance, and economic structures and systems can be evolved only if we develop people with the capacity to be whole by achieving their potential.

Currently, the ways we raise children and foster their success as adults are based on outdated, even archaic, paradigms of human development. The machine and behavioral view of humans conditions us to believe that we cannot know ourselves and must rely on others—including parents, teachers, supervisors, legislators, and judges—to make sense of our behavior and tell us what is right. We manage people with feedback, firmly believing that external input is the only way to get the results we want. We do not build into our systems the practices necessary for development of ableness and personal mastery and discourage people from appreciating their potential, let alone ever actualizing it.

Picture for a moment the powerful role that businesses play in limiting the development of all but the a few designated high-performers, and then visualize the power of giving every employee the capacity for self-direction, self-assessment, and self-correction. The benefits of taking on the challenge of developmental alternatives to toxic business practices cannot be overestimated. And finally, imagine the wonder of living in a world where "achieving my full potential" was the only accepted incentive for working, and everyone was fully able to make more meaningful contributions every day of their lives.

Third, to accept our instrumental role in regenerating ecosystems. The mandate to regenerate our radically altered ecosystems rests on working societies and development of the full potential of every living person. We have created many scattered movements for evolving toward a vital and viable Earth but we are not yet thinking systemically. A vast majority of us have not learned to engage as living beings with other living beings in regenerative processes. And as a result, we have not yet developed the capacity to work developmentally and holistically on the largest scale.

Feedback has taught us to look for what is literally visible—the physical and the functional—rather than watch for how dynamic systems change in the larger, whole living systems in which we dwell. Every place on Earth is unique and alive. Imagine the magnitude of change if entire organizations and industries across a nation took up the challenge of developmental transformation. And then imagine the power we could bring to restoring Earth's living systems.

It is not a quick and easy step to imagine. Yet that same living, systemic thinking process is exactly what is needed to understand how markets work and see where we can engage with customers in our markets. Nor is it possible to know in advance how each human being in an organization will stretch to serve those customers in a well-structured, ongoing, holistic process that is developing their capabilities and capturing markets. But feedback is one of the hurdles over which we must leap if we are to achieve this level of clear thinking.

Feedback processes are unnecessary. If we fully develop the capacities for self-reflection and self-assessment (locus of control, scope of consideration, and source of agency), then we are more than able to manage our behavior and develop living systems thinking skills and personal mastery. What a contorted process we have created to fix a developmental shortfall, and for all our effort we still have not accomplished the intended aim.

There is a direct path, easier but still not easy, to the development of each and every one of us. We and all of our organizations, smallest to largest, are perfectly suited to do this work, to reap its benefits, and to expand its scope to the level of whole planet. In this way, if you add to a working society and fully realized humans the ability to act together in partnership with global processes, you truly bring forward the potential for our species to play a role in the regeneration of Earth. From the perspective of today's business-as-usual attitude, this seems like a daunting aspiration. Most of us cannot imagine an immediate connection to out-of-balance natural processes in any ongoing way. But if we take what is working in us and begin to imagine, articulate, and develop our core human capacities, the biggest transformation of all is possible.

The Easier but Still Not Easy Path

It is a hard road, to go against prevailing paradigms and the assurances we are given that everything will work out in the end. But trust me. Developing discernment and the core capacities is difficult, destabilizing, and almost impossible to accomplish alone. The most effective path has proven to be working regularly and intensely with others in similar positions, those who are also questioning, reconceptualizing, and then designing out feedback and other toxic practices. The way forward is not simply to adopt a new practice. First, we must shift mental paradigms.

James Edward and Zac: My Own Proof of the Pudding

Can moving from feedback and other toxic practices to a developmental approach work when all else has failed? It already has. Consider the happy ending to my own feedback experience. Then there is the story of what happened when Bob Casey, a DuPont executive preparing for retirement, wanted to do something about troubling issues in his North Delaware community.

Casey founded an organization called Creative Grandparenting as a way to take what he learned about developmental approaches to transformation at DuPont into the inner city. The original mission was to educate community elders to work with youth—one or both of whose parents were dead, in halfway houses or jail—in order to give them a better chance at a good life.

Creative Parenting did well and was awarded ongoing funding by the state of Delaware to serve more communities. With this step up, the program became so successful that it won a National Governors Association award for advancing the lives of underprivileged children. Soon other states approached Casey and his organization, asking them to help spread the powerful effects of their work beyond Delaware.

It had been my role at the founding of CP and in its early days to lead the design of mentor curriculum and training, and so Casey asked me to become involved in the expansion. Working on the West Coast where I lived made sense, and so did upgrading the curriculum for the next evolution of the mission. I began in California, partnering with the state Department of Community Services and Development, then directed by Jim Stokes. For the inaugural program, Stokes chose Fullerton, one of the state's toughest communities due to its high levels of poverty and gang activity.

We met with a group of young men in their twenties who were ex-gang members. They were mentored by volunteers from the business community; in return, they agreed to mentor kids in middle and early high school. Our initial interactions seemed confusing to them. The answers they gave to my questions were clearly what they thought I wanted to hear or what they wanted to make sure that I knew. In response, I asked them more questions, giving them space to think before they answered. All of these questions were intended to elicit self-reflection as a way to enable them to discover and articulate their own experiences.

One young man, who called himself "Conan" after the fictional pirate, de- manded to know what I thought of his answers and then what I thought of him. It took a couple of weeks with Conan before he realized that I was not going to share any of my thoughts. It took a bit longer for him to understand that he did not need to try to position himself relative to my impressions. It was after I had met with him every few weeks for six months, resourcing his mentoring of a 13-year-old middle schooler named Zac, that he brought me a wonderful story.

Conan reported he had been spending a lot of time correcting Zac's behaviors, such as lying and cheating, that he thought would lead to gang behavior. He was catching out Zac as quickly as he could and correcting him, and he loved being looked up to by the younger boy. This kind of tough discipline is how Conan had been raised. He knew it had not stopped his own slide into gang life so he added lots of positive feedback when Zac behaved well, and Zac worked hard to get it.

Conan was gratified by this up to the moment when he realized that he was making the affirmations not for Zac but for himself. He had been experimenting with the ideas in the curriculum, which included not evaluating or giving advice or feedback to the mentee. This approach had been difficult for Conan because it contradicted what he craved and had missed as a child—positive feedback and admiration. Nevertheless, he decided to take the curriculum seriously and try something different.

He shifted to what he called an "SP" role (i.e. Socratic method), asking Zac what he thought about his behaviors and experiences. Conan struggled internally to stay on track but he persevered. He told Zac that he should rely on his own thoughts and ideas and not adopt anyone else's, and he refused to succumb to Zac's highly exaggerated good behavior, which sought his approval.

Conan told me that after a month of this practice, Zac offered a reflection on something in himself that he understood was less than positive. Conan's first instinct was to jump in and give advice. But, he proudly reported, he had bitten his tongue and instead started asking questions, hoping that Zac would find his own way and move toward a plan. For more than an hour, long past their scheduled 20-minute session, Conan helped Zac reflect and examine his own thoughts. Zac was small for his age but Conan said that he was large in terms of his determination. When Zac finally got an idea for a plan, a little one but entirely his own, Conan ended the session promising to check in the next day. Nervous when he called, he was shocked to hear that Zac was excited because of what he had observed in himself as he tried out his idea on his parents.

It was not long before Zac became less dependent on Conan's ideas, and he now shared his own thinking. Whenever Conan seemed about to give him advice, Zac would stop him and demand more of those "good questions." He insisted that Conan let him figure it out for himself.

Conan wanted to tell me this story because he had figured out why I would not tell him how he was doing or what he should think or do. Conan also began asking his own volunteer mentor for questions instead of advice. He told me that his girlfriend was pregnant and wondered how he could learn to parent this way.

You could have bowled me over, I was so taken back.

I started pushing Conan for deeper and more thoughtful responses to hard questions and situations. I refused to answer his questions but asked him to examine them using the systemic frameworks. He never backed down. He told me the last time the class met that he had changed his name back to James Edward after his two grandfathers because he no longer wanted to think of himself as a pirate. He never knew them but he was asking questions about them and beginning to see them as role models. Zac had moved to another school district and would no longer be in the program, but James Edward said he was going to keep track of him because Zac had given him so much that he wanted to "get even with him" in the best possible way by continuing to ask him the hard questions.

———————

The last thing I ever heard from James Edward was a short reflection he made in a video used to promote the program to other school districts. "Thinking for yourself is the only way to be on the straight and narrow." James Edward had learned to think for himself. Not a bad return, multiplied by all the others who came through the program successfully.

This experience was for me the perfect, final antidote to my experience with feedback 20 years earlier at San Jose State University. I now knew once and for all that my decision to leave my department was the right one. It launched me on my path to seek out and share alternatives to the toxic practices that undermine us as children, students, employees, leaders, and developers of other human beings. I hope that this short examination of feedback and its alternative will further you and your organization on your own developmental paths.

CONNECT TO A DEVELOPMENTAL LEADERSHIP COMMUNITY

NEWSLETTER—carolsanford.com

Periodic updates and recommendations from Carol Sanford, including readings and announcements of events, interviews, and Carol's guest blogs on other platforms.

PODCASTS AND BLOGS

Business Second Opinion Blog and *Podcast* (carolsanford. com*)*, a contrarian view of best business best practices as espoused in *Harvard Business Review* and other popular journals, along with alternatives that work from the Regenerative Paradigm and Regenerative Business Education. Opinions and ideas offered by Carol Sanford with Zac Swartout as host.

The Responsible Capitalist (carolsafordinstitute.com), interviews with investors who want their financial engagement to make a difference.

The Regenerative Business (carolsafordinstitute.com), interviews with business leaders pursuing regenerative principles, imperfectly but with discipline to evolve, built on the foundation of Regenerative Business Education.

THE REGENERATIVE BUSINESS DEVELOPMENT COMMUNITY—carolsanfordinstitute.com

Live, webinar-based, multi-company series, with eight online presentations and additional focused work with individual companies by a member of The Regenerative Business Alliance. Year One: Strategic Direction. Year Two: Industry Leadership. Year Three: Work Design and People Management. Offered on a revolving basis; can be taken in any sequence.

THE REGENERATIVE BUSINESS EXECUTIVE BOOK CLUB—carolsanford.com/executive-plus-book-club

THE REGENERATIVE SEED-COMMUNITIES—seed-communities.com

For change agents and global change agents.

BOOKS BY CAROL SANFORD—carolsanford.com

The Regenerative Business: Redesign Work. Cultivate Human Potential. Achieve Extraordinary Outcomes, Nicholas Brealey Press 2017. Hardcover, Audible, and digital editions. Bulk Discounts of up to 50 percent and additional bonuses also available.

The Responsible Business: Reimagining Sustainability and Success, Jossey-Bass: A Wiley Imprint, 2011. Hardcover, softcover, Audible, and digital editions.

The Responsible Entrepreneur: Four Game-Changing Arche-

types for Founders, Leaders, and Impact Investors. Jossey-Bass: A Wiley Imprint. Hardcover, softcover, Audible, and digital editions.

Carol Sanford on Social Media

Medium—medium.com/@carolsanford

LinkedIn—linkedin.com/in/carolsanfordkeynote

Facebook—facebook.com/carol.sanford2

Twitter—twitter.com/carolsanford

Endnotes

1   This book, *The Toxic Effects of Feedback and Its Developmental Alternative*, is the first in a series, The Toxic Practices, which will explore a few of the most prevalent management practices and their negative effects on businesses and other organizations, people in businesses and organizations, and all of us, in general. The series will also present alternative ways of thinking, working, and living together. For a partial list of the toxic practices, see Carol Sanford, *The Regenerative Business: Redesign Work, Cultivate Human Potential, Achieve Extraordinary Outcomes* (Boston and London: Nicholas Brealey Publishing, 2017).

2   The following sketch of the three core human capacities is excerpted from Carol Sanford, *The Regenerative Business: Redesign Work, Cultivate Human Potential, Achieve Extraordinary Outcomes*.

3   Feedback (n.d.) in *Wikipedia*, accessed September 5, 2018, https://en.wikipedia.org/wiki/Feedback.

4   Feedback (n.d.) in *Wikipedia*, accessed September 5, 2018, https://en.wikipedia.org/wiki/Feedback.

5   Macy conferences (n.d.) in *Wikipedia*, accessed September 5, 2018, https://en.wikipedia.org/wiki/Macy_conferences.

6   Steve Joshua Heims (2018) at The MIT Press, accessed May 9, 2018, https://mitpress.mit.edu/contributors/steve-joshua-heims.

7   History of Cybernetics, Chapter 2: The Coalescence of Cybernetics (2016) at Applying the Science of Context, accessed May 17, 2018 http://www.asc-cybernetics.org/foundations/history2.htm #MacySum.

8   History of Cybernetics, Chapter 2: The Coalescence of Cybernetics (2016) at Applying the Science of Context, accessed May 17, 2018 http://www.asc-cybernetics.org/foundations/history2.htm #MacySum.

9   For a complete list of participants at the Macy Conferences on Cybernetics and links to further information: accessed May 17, 2018: http://www.asc-cybernetics.org/foundations/history/MacyPeople.htm.

10   What Is Whole Brain Thinking (1981-2015) at Herrmann, accessed June 1, 2018, http://www.herrmannsolutions.com/what-is-whole-brain-thinking-2/.

11   Raising Independent Kids and Self-Directed Learners (2014) at Happiness Is Here, accessed September 5, 2018, http://happinessishereblog.com/2014/09/raising-independent-kids-and-self-directed-learners/.

12   For more information: 10 Cognitive Biases that Distort Your Mind (2018) at Very Well Mind, accessed September 5, 2018, https://www.verywellmind.com/cognitive-biases-distort-thinking-2794763.

13   Norbert Wiener, *The Human Use of Human Beings: Cybernetics and Society* (Boston: Da Capo Press, 1988).

14   Karl Ludwig von Bertalanffy, *General Systems Theory: Foundations, Development, Applications* (New York: Geroge Braziller, 1968).

15   John G. Bennett, *Energies: Material, Vital, Cosmic* (Gloucestershire, England: Coombe Springs Press, 1964).

16   Wiener1988.

17   von Bertalanffy 1968; Ervin Laszlo (editor), *The New Evolutionary Paradigm* (New York: Gordon and Beach, 1991); James G. Miller, *Living Systems* (New York: McGraw Hill Books, 1978).

18   Gregory Bateson, *Mind and Nature* (New York: E. P. Dutton, 1979).

19   Charles Krone, in private conversations and dialogues in Carmel, CA, from 1977 to 2014.

20   David Bohm, *Wholeness and the Implicate Order* (London: Routledge and Kegan Paul, 1980); Douglas R. Hofstadter and Daniel C. Dennett, *The Mind's Eye: Fantasies and Reflections on Self and Soul* (New York: Basic Books, 1981); Ilya Prigogine and Isabelle Stengers, *Order Out of Chaos* (New York: Bantam Books, 1984); Karl Pribram, "Problems Concerning the Structure

of Consciousness" in Gordon Globus (editor), *Consciousness and the Brain: A Scientific and Philosophical Inquiry* (New York: Plenum Press, 1976).

21 For an extensive description of the new soap business headquartered in Lima, see Carol Sanford, *The Responsible Business: Reimaging Sustainability and Success* (San Francisco: Jossey-Bass, 2011).

22 Carol Sanford, "Business and Education: Some Uncommon Sense About Learning," a Springhill Publications Occasional Paper (Battle Ground, Washington, 1993).

23 At the time, the Freon trademark belonged to DuPont; it has since changed hands and now belongs to Dow Chemical.

24 Sanford 2011.

25 See Sanford 2017 for a list of 30 toxic practices fundamental to most current work designs that undermine individual success and create a false idea of high-level performance.

26 The Proudfoot practice is an offering of Management Consulting Group, PLC, founded by Alexander Proudfoot.

27 See Sanford 2017, chapters 7-12, for the five phases of changeover to systems-based work design.

28 Charles Krone 1977 to 2014. Krone developed the concept of *developmental organization* and conveyed it to a small cadre of resources in his membership community. What follows here is based on the author's understanding of his teaching.

29 Sanford 2017.

30 Jeffrey Hollender, "How I Did It: Giving Up the CEO Seat, *Harvard Business Review*, March 2010.

31 See also Sanford 2011 and Carol Sanford, *The Responsible Entrepreneur: Four Game-Changing Archetypes for Founders, Leaders, and Impact Investors* (San Francisco: Jossey-Bass, 2014).

32 Herb Meyer, Emanuel Kay, and John R. P. French, "Split Roles in Performance Appraisal," *Harvard Business Review*, January 1965.

33 Douglas McGregor, "An Uneasy Look at Performance Appraisal," *Harvard Business Review*, September 1972.

Made in the USA
Coppell, TX
08 December 2022

88104632R00111